T0367612

Philpott Church Hamilton

Memorable Moments from My Early Childhood to Adulthood to Refugee Camp-Ghana, West Africa, and unto Hamilton City-Ontario-Canada

After coming to Canada, I faced many challenges in life. When I was in a refugee camp, I prayed for God to help me find a church when I arrived in Canada with my family. God answered my prayers when we successfully made our departure to Canada and became members of the Philpott Memorial Church in Hamilton, Ontario, Canada, 2005.

I grew up in a small village in Liberia and later moved to Bentol in Western Civilization. An angelic woman named Jemima Thompson-Parker rescued me from the streets and took me in as her own, which was a life-changing moment for me. This experience prompted me to become a human rights activist in my community, and I began volunteering with seniors after finishing high school, at age 21.

One of my most significant spiritual moments was when Mrs. Jemima Parker organized a meeting to change my name out of love at age 10. With the guidance of the Holy Spirit, my childhood name changed from "Brandy" to "Isaac Alexander Yoryor-III." My late Mrs. Parker asserts, "I couldn't carry a Liquor name." Our late father, Cousin George Parker, and my brother, M. Dave Parker, attended the meeting." This was a significant and spiritual experience for me, and I hold it close to my heart as a cherished memory from my childhood in Bentol, Liberia.

GIVING LIFE
A MEANING

EYE WITNESS ACCOUNTS OF THE LIBERIAN CIVIL WAR
THE EMOTIONS THAT FOLLOWS AFTER THE WAR
EXPOSURES OF GRIEVOUS EVIL

ISAAC ALEX YORYOR, III

WESTBOW
PRESS®
A DIVISION OF THOMAS NELSON
& ZONDERVAN

WestBow Press books may be ordered through booksellers or by contacting:

WestBow Press
A Division of Thomas Nelson & Zondervan
1663 Liberty Drive
Bloomington, IN 47403
www.westbowpress.com
844-714-3454

New International Version, NIV Holy Bible, New International Version®, NIV® Copyright ©1973, 1978, 1984, 2011 by Biblica, Inc.® Used by permission. All rights reserved worldwide

ISBN: 979-8-3850-1011-0 (sc)
ISBN: 979-8-3850-1012-7 (e)

Print information available on the last page.

WestBow Press rev. date: 08/01/2024

Contents

Giving Life A Meaning

"In this book, Isaac Yoryor recounts the horrors of the Liberian Civil War, his dangerous journey escaping the war, and the subsequent 14 years he spent living in a series of dangerous and notorious refugee camps. Isaac and his family eventually found refuge in Canada and settled in Hamilton, Ontario. Throughout the book, Isaac speaks about the ways he was sustained by God in his journey, the meanings he learned about life, and the actions we need to take as humankind to prevent the types of horrors he and others faced in the future."

Dr. Gary Dumbrill (A Great Mentor!)
Associate Professor, Social Work
Faculty of Social Sciences, McMaster
University-Hamilton-Ontario-Ca.

DEDICATION

This book is dedicated to my foster parents, the late Mr. and Mrs. Jamima Thompson Parker, for their love and care and for giving me a good education and work ethic, teaching me about honesty, good Christian values, and concepts of God. My late parents, especially my father, spent much time during my early age taking me from family to family for help in getting me an education. Daddy, though tragically taken away by evil men, I appreciate and cherish your efforts.

Also, to the thousands of innocent lives lost during the Liberian Civil War in 1990. Those who managed to escape to exile but did not make it; some tragically died, while others died of different diseases for spiritual reasons. May these souls rest in the bosom of God. I am also pleased to dedicate this project to my children's educational funds.

ACKNOWLEDGMENTS

I sincerely thank my former English as Second Language (ESL) instructor, Ronald Berenbaum, for his courage in reviewing my manuscript; my Canadian dad, Larry McDonald; and my friend Rick Bradford and his family, the first contributors to this work. My dear former pastor Lane Fusilier and family; Philpott Memorial Church's Tuesday Morning Men Group; and Professor Gary Dumbrill (McMaster University School of Social Work), Dr. Archibald Stuart (Surgeon), the late Patricia T. Harvey (Ophthalmologists), for their courage, spiritual, financial, and moral support. Thanks to the hard-working family at WestBow Press, a division of Thomas Nelson, Ltd. Importantly, I'd like to thank my dear wife, Evelyn; my five daughters, Valerie, Alexis, Rita, Islyn, and Andriel; my eight grandchildren, Miracle, Bob Isaac, Francis, Michael, Irvan, Dior, Belle, Omari, and my son, Daddy Boy Yoryor. I would also like to thank the late Bryan Wylie, with whom I initially discussed putting my stories together. His encouragement played a significant role in beginning this work. My dearest sister, Ida Y. Parker, was instrumental in resettling abroad from the refugee camp in Ghana through her great concern for my future. Thank God for her courage in replacing our dead parents. And my dearest sister-in-law, Mrs. Etmonia G. Moore, for her tremendous emotional and financial support toward us in the refugee camp in Ghana.

The United States, Britain, and the International Community

I would also love to extend my utmost thanks and appreciation to the Economic Community of West African States (ECOWAS), the United Nations, the African Union (AU), the United States, Britain, and other nations around the world that helped to find peace and stop the bloodshed in Liberia and significant financial contributions for its reconstruction.

INTRODUCTION

This book addresses philosophical questions about the purpose and meaning of life and existence. In this sense, the concepts collected in this book deal with various related questions, such as "Why are we here?" "What is life about?" and, "What is the meaning of all this?" And, "Why should anyone take it away?" This book attempts to answer these questions. I saw evil unfold, a melodrama, and the narratives about the fourteen years-long civil war in the West African state of Liberia, founded by free slaves in 1820. As I started to write my stories in 2011, tears ran down my cheeks like a mighty torrent. I recorded the horrors and the decomposed bodies of children, the elderly, pregnant women, and bodies as the result of revenge killings.

The meaning of life is intermingled with religious understandings, God, and his existence, social bonds, consciousness, and happiness. I uncovered the meaning of life touches on many other topics, such as values, purposes, ethics, good and evil, and free will.

This book bases its arguments on my personal experiences and data collected during the civil war in my native Liberia. It includes the dramatic changes that occurred in my life, including fourteen years spent in one of the largest refugee camps in Africa. In this refugee camp, people awaited the opportunity to escape dire, humiliating circumstances. When Canada opened its doors to us, it was as if they had sent life boats to rescue our drowning souls. I hope readers will sympathize with the thousands of immigrants and refugees who have experienced massive discrimination, excruciating pain, suffering, and slaughter at the hands of their people. However, history often has a bittersweet side, and to that end, I also recount my humorous migration to Canada. Canada is known for being one of the world's most peaceful and warmest-hearted nations. The Canadian citizens began showing their love when I entered its borders. There is hope in Canada, and refugees like me love and appreciate our new country.

Life will be meaningless if you don't find meaning in it. When you finish reading this book, I hope you understand the social problems and emotional issues that those in my circumstances face daily. We must encourage and teach each other; a light is at the end of the tunnel. Don't just sit there. Get up. Also, if you work to remove obstacles holding you back, your life can find meaning. But it won't happen overnight; it takes courage and persistence. In this book, you will read about my early life, and how I overcame the circumstances I was born into. It was a good idea to share personal experiences that changed my life. As strengths, I reinforce courage and persistence through life transitions. I also present observations on the cultural differences immigrants and refugees must navigate when they arrive in their new countries with vast dreams. It means many immigrants and refugees, like me and my family, suffered persecution in their native countries. In Liberia, my fellow citizens were emotionally deeply deprived of their birth homes and sustained the need for necessities. Thank God Canada, the United States, and other industrialized countries have invested millions of dollars to resettle refugees. Canada is one of the most peaceful countries in the world; the United States, among the world's nations, is the most liberal. Both the United States and Canada have immense respect for human rights.

There are also tragic and inspiring stories in this book that illustrate how the rewards in one's life change depending on how one lives. The people who live life well will surely reap the rewards. Writing this book has inspired me more than ever to continue serving my church, family, community, and especially the refugee community. Finally, in my conclusion, I peruse issues of the bone that never found a resting place. (Disclaimer: all credits on all historicity of the founding of Liberia go to the United States Library of Congress)

ONE

Born in Extreme Poverty

I WAS BORN into a very poor family. My family survived on subsistence farming and eating rodents caught in rattraps; we had one meal a day, mostly during the evening hours. We couldn't afford to buy a rattrap from the stores, so we had to prepare traditionally made traps for the rats. A typical African rat trap takes about one hour or more to prepare; it depends on how many traps you want. The process starts by using a special flexible stick found in the bushes of Africa's tropical forests. The stick needs to be just about twenty-four and a half feet long and is bent into a Ushape, braided with palm leaves, and daubed with clay mud. It weighs about ten to fifteen pounds. You then plant another U-shaped stick in the ground. A rope is attached to a sharp edge of bambooat the top end of the daubed trap. To complete the trap, you raise the front of the daubed trap four to five inches high and hook it to the U-shaped stick planted in the ground. The trigger is plugged with a wrapped palm nut. Rats are sensitive to the smells of wrapped palm nuts, so they're effective in setting a rattrap.

The entire process of preparing a rattrap and at the same time being on alert for snakebites is very stressful. In addition to snakebites, you must deal with thorns, saw grass, cuts from wild yam vines, and yellow jacket stings. You are also overshadowed by the fear of hungry boars.

After setting the traps, you must get up as early as four or five o'clock every morning and search the traps for catches. Sadly, there are days you may come home without a catch from any of the traps.

I was raised in a tiny village consisting of five huts roofed with palm, or piassava leaves. I stayed in the village until I was eight years old. Then, my father began looking for a family I could live with. He realized the importance of an education and did not want all five of his children to grow up in a meager village. His plan was for me to do domestic work for the family. In return for my services, the family would send me to school.

I would describe my village life as living one day at a time. Survival depended on what happened daily. Bare foot children ran around the town amid the excrement of domestic animals like country chickens, goats, dogs, cows, and wild rats. Mosquito bites could lead to malaria. The nightly entertainment of annoying, squeaking mosquitoes led to restless nightly sleep. I and the rest of the children in the village had no idea we were in danger of contracting diseases from the filth we were exposed to daily. Whenever any of us or others in the village got ill, our parents gave us traditional herbs to drink, which came from tree bark and other leaves from the bushes. These traditional medications had no scientific measurements. Subsequently, on my arrival in the West and after spending a few semesters in medical school, I realized the importance of giving medications according to age, weight, medical history, and diagnosis. However, in our village, none of those medical requirements we reconsidered. Despite the sordid conditions, people survived.

After leaving the village for urban civilization and water was piped, treated, and made drinkable, I wondered how I'd survived those years of drinking from contaminated and polluted creeks and streams. When it rained, all the human and animal excrement ran into the stream and contaminated the water we drank. We used the same stream to wash clothes, cook, and take our daily showers. After my exposure to Western life, I often lamented about how the village seemed like a dreadful dream in which terrible and unexpected things happened regularly.

My father and I circled many families in search of educational opportunities for me. I remember two families. The first was the Woodson family from a town called Caresburg, Montserrado County, Liberia. This family was wealthy. As a child from the village, everything seemed admirable to me. The second family was headed by Mr. Freeman, a well-respected teacher noted for being a disciplinarian. My father believed these families had values I could benefit from. Our parents could not afford to send us to school; and my father tried his best to get me and the rest of my brothers and sisters into a school. However, I wasn't interested in going to school. When I thought about school, it reminded me of caning, a painful punishment meted out within the African school system by teachers in which the child was struck forcefully with a cane. The use of canes is very common in our culture; most African/Liberian teachers believe in caning for the child to learn. Many schoolchildren in my village avoided school because of the use of caning.

Even though I'd lost interest in school at the time, my father did not give up on his goal to have me educated. At first, his plan did not work out. Destiny finally landed me in the city of Bentol, Liberia. I'd traveled there with my grandmother, whom we called "Old Lady-Gartaye." She was actually my father's elder sister, but because we never saw any of our grandparents and never enjoyed the comfort of our grandparents, she was the only one we knew as a grandma. My father was known by family members as Yoryor Teemgbae, and my biological mother, Ma Larcee Mehzoah-Yoryor. She also hails from Nimba County, and from a town named: Gblo-Diala. My dead and living siblings: John K. Yoryor(Late), Samuel Yoryor(Late), Peter G. Yoryor(late),two sisters: Jessica Yoryor(USA), Catherine Yoryor(Liberia). One Aunt: Aunty Cecelia. My father started his early life as a traditional singer. My father was hired by villages in the region to sing at annual traditional festivals. Chapter two details my exit from an extreme impoverish village life to the city.

TWO

A Journey to My Destiny

THE DAY I left the village was complex and challenging. I ran after the vehicle that had taken me and my grandmother to Bentol City, Liberia. I ran after the car for approximately forty-five minutes. As a child, I didn't realize it was a journey to my destiny. A family friend, Mr. Babyboy Woodson, hired my traditional herbalist grandmother to perform a traditional ritual on his mini-diamond mine in Bentol City. A traditional African herbalist possesses the gifts and abilities to see beyond the ordinary. It's believes in many African cultures and traditions that diamonds are preserved and controlled by supernatural spiritual-powers refers to by Liberians as "Ginah." I wore only the soiled clothing I was wearing when I arrived.

I was only ten years old when I came to Bentol Cityin 1973 and was fortunate to connect with my adoptive family. When we got to the city, I quickly found friends I ran around with. One day while playing near the home of the Parker-Thompson family, the woman who would become my second mother on earth, Mrs. Jemima Thompson-Parker, asked me, "Who are your parents? Who do you live with?"

"My grandmother," I told her.

She asked me to come along with my grandmother to her home the following day. I was excited because the Parker-Thompsons were one of the middle-class families in the city. They had a car, which meant she was wealthy compared to the rest of the townspeople. I was instantly drawn to the car because I'd rarely seen one while growing up in a village.

My grandmother walked me to Mrs. Thompson-Parker's home early the following day. Mrs. Parker asked my grandmother if I could stay with her family, and she promised to send me to school.

My grandmother paused and looked at Mrs. Parker. "He is your son now," my grandmother said.

Then, my grandma started to do her appreciative traditional dance and sang in the local Liberian language (Dahn Tribes of Northern Liberia. The song entitled in Dahn as: "Jesah-Ko-lah," means: "Jesus Blesses Us Bountifully"). She lamented to Mrs. Parker, "All my brother's children stay in the village with no opportunities for education."

At this point in my early childhood, I found a new home in the city. I was placed in first grade, but since it was the middle of the semester, I had to learn the ABCs on flashcards at home while waiting for the second semester to begin (I would love thank my foster brother Alvin H. Porte, Jr. for being my early childhood Tutor).

Getting ready for the next semester of school was not an easy start. I learned with the cane on the buttocks, but I endured all the penalties. I never understood why I was willing to take so much punishment, but something kept me going. Friends in the community always tried to discourage me by telling me to run away and go to my birth parents in the village. I met a family friend named "Uncle-Joseph." He came from the same town where I grew up. Whenever I complained to him and asked him to take me home to my parents, he always responded with divine advice, encouraging me to endure. Uncle Joseph always reminded me of where I came from and assured me of good results in the future if I stayed and exercised patience. He compared my life with those who tried to discourage me. He told me that if I listened to them, I would end up like them—an adult without education.

As I grew older, I often wondered, *would life have had the same meaning if I had followed the bad advice from my friends?* The true strength of my new family came from the Word of God. We always had prayers on Sunday mornings, before preparing for church services. I will never forget the smell of freshly baked cornbread made with Blue Band margarine. During regular Sunday morning prayers, I occasionally crept out to check on the bread in the charcoal oven. I was sure everyone's eyes were closed before checking on the cornbread. This is an excellent memory for me because it represents leaving the extreme poverty of my village and entering civilization. Everything interested me, especially food. Sometimes, I experimented with everything in my new life because everything was incredible. The next chapter details issues of honesty as I transitioned from the village civilization and this new way of life.

THREE

Passing through the Furnace of Honesty

A S I GREW into my teens, our adoptive parents taught us family values and love for God. These values included being devoted and honest and continuously worshipping God. I wasn't allowed to tell lies or cheat. There were no options to be an "eye servant," meaning to give birth to hypocrisy. My mother used to say, "The truth shall set you free." Our mother was the treasure at the McIntosh Grove United Methodist Church, Bentol City, Liberia, before she died in 1988 after a catastrophic illness.

I lived with the Thompson-Parkers until I graduated from high school in 1984. My first two daughters, Valerie and Alexis, were born in 1983 and 1984. Having these two girls took work. Our father warned us not to have a child before the right time. However, as a teenager, falling in love was a new experience. Of course, teenagers would not listen to their parents' advice. I was in eleventh grade when Rosemarie Blake, the mother of my two oldest daughters, and I had Valerie. Shortly after, she became pregnant with Alexis. I never realized what I was up against until I ascended to twelfth grade and already had two small children.

While attending school, I also did a difficult job. I cut trees used to produce charcoal. It was physically exhausting, but I needed the money for baby food and other necessities. These memories scarred my heart and made me want to cry whenever I remembered the horrible experiences. Sometimes, I felt like crying, but the tears would not come out. I often felt the pain and memories and screaming internally. Imagine that proceeds from the sales of the charcoal were to enable me to buy baby food. At one point, I lost a hundred bags of charcoal due to a hidden fire in one of the bags of coal. The offer scenario generated unimaginable feelings and frustrations.

A mother's love is something essential to experience both as a child and then as an adult. I remember my mother, Jemima, was very sorry for me and often gave me money to buy food for my baby girls. Our family had great times of unity and love, even though our lives were not 'milk and honey.'

Mrs. Parker was treasurer at McIntosh Grove United Methodist Church in Bentol, Liberia. She often entrusted me with money from the church. I also ran the family retail store between the ages of ten and twelve. From 1986 to 1990, I worked as the general manager of a trading company that supplied retailers in Monrovia, Liberia's capital. When I went to the settlement on weekends, my mother would call me into her room and spend an hour advising me on money management. "Keep your hands off other people's money," she said. "Be satisfied with what is yours." She lamented, "Money represents good and evil." She advised me that when people trust you, you have that asset for life. Even today, those words ring in my ears. As a married man with a family, I tried to instill these values in my children.

Before the war in Liberia, I worked with Nyongbae Trading Company, owned by a Liberian businessman named Tugbeh N. Doe. Mr. Doe once told me, "By being so honest with me, count on me for recommendations for work as long as I live." This promise "for life" was something I always appreciated and valued. He taught me to believe how vital honesty is in life. Mr. Doe died in Liberia in 2023.

Our family had great unity and love, even though our lives were not milk and honey. Our parents taught us good moral values. We were not allowed to smoke cigarettes, drink alcohol, or be friends with people who used drugs. We had to live under some strange rules. For example, if they saw us wearing sunglasses, our mother would call us and ask us to take off our sunglasses so she could have a look at the color of our eyes; users of street drugs and alcohol were recognized by changes in the redness of their eyes. There was no segregation in our family. We all shared the same housework on the farm and in the yard.

The gifts from our mother we shared equally with everyone else. We shared our clothes and went to the same school. There were stories of other families who segregated their biological children from the ones they raised as foster children.

I was always available for work in the garden. Our adoptive father, the late George A. Parker, Sr., saw that I was a hard worker with intelligence and assigned me to a small family distillery that produced cane juice, "juice of cane" as it was referred to in our local vernacular, a sugarcane alcoholic beverage sold in local markets. Part of my responsibilities was to feed the pigs. I got attached to feeding the pigs and the dogs. It was fascinating and fun to feed the animals. They recognized me from a distance and would begin to scream when they realized I was around because it meant it was time to eat!

Pigs are stubborn animals, but every animal knows if someone loves it. They knew my voice; even if I didn't speak, they would smell me from a distance and start whining. And they would roar to let me know they were hungry. The pigs and I became friends. It was challenging for me when it came time to slaughter the pigs to sell the meat. I sometimes cried knowing my friends the pigs would be killed. We sold pork every Saturday at the market. We never had a problem selling pork meat because our community was 100 percent Christian; we never had a problem with other religions because we sold pork. I used my salary to buy my school uniforms.

After graduating from high school, I wanted to attend the university. I wrote a lovely letter to my adoptive parents, thanking them for the care and support they had given me. And I indicated that I wanted to pursue higher educational goals.

"My son, your mom and dad love you," Mother Jemima replied.

We have tried to express our love in many ways. We are delighted and proud that you want to continue your education. Unfortunately, I am not well and no longer as strong as before. In addition, we have had some financial setbacks, and things are tougher on us. We would love to continue helping you with your education; we can't do it now. You have become intelligent and growing into manhood and hardworking, and we know that you will be able to find a way to continue your education. Our prayers go with you.

I found Mom's words to be an inspiration. Then I found out that she had kidney disease, which was getting worse. As a result, she had to spend more time in the hospital, which was an emotional moment. Over the years, I promised myself that I would repay my mother for all the good things she did for me. In particular, I promised I would take care of her when she was old. Our mother was hospitalized for several months with a severe kidney problem at age sixty-five. Her only hope of survival was a transplant, but the financial resources weren't available.

In Liberia after the 1980 coup d'état, there was nothing like government-provided healthcare to cover the cost of my mother's surgery. The procedure would have cost our family over $50,000. We didn't have that amount of available money. At the time, I was earning only about 130 Liberian dollars per month, less than $50 Canadian.

My sister Evangeline came to my workplace whenever Mom needed some stuff in the hospital. Whenever she ran out of supplies at the hospital, Mom sent Evangeline to inform me that all her supplies ran out. I would be overwhelmed with sadness. I can remember a particular moment in our relationship. It was a time of regret, sadness, and never-ending tears. There are good and a bad time in the life of every family, and my goal has always been to give life meaning whenever I can.

Chapter 4 details the emotions of death, the loss of a loving mother, and how the journeys of life start with motherly love and care. I believe it comes first in the hospital, or in Africa, behind the mud house and traditional midwives. Mothers are the true epitome of giving life meaning in the lives of every child up to adulthood.

FOUR

Life is Meaningless without Parental Love

INVADED BY DEEP pain, I spent many nights shedding tears for her. She often said, "I hope I live long enough to see you become a lawyer." She thought I would be a good lawyer because of how I interacted with other family members. I usually won family arguments and was generally successful in influencing the good behaviors of other family members. I often had the last word when it came to solving the domestic problems of our home.

My mom had gotten sick when I was considering going to college. It was a big problem since she was the source of income for the whole family. I always felt there was something special about this family. My parents did not practice favoritism among us. Biological children and non-biological children receive the same deal.

I remember only a few acts of favoritism toward biological children, which were probably only oversights. We were receptive to each other because we all treated each other equally. This type of family management could serve as a good role model for foster homes and caregivers in Africa and worldwide. It is a model that creates bonds, which produce good roots. Good roots usually have good fruit.

The family lived by Christian principles, which made us create a strong family bond. "Christian principles" means an individual, a family, or a group of people who establish their religious values based on Christian beliefs and biblical teachings. Jemima Parker's family produced six gospel preachers, including Monroe, and our late brother, Konah Parker. One of my brothers, Monroe, is working on his doctorate in ministry. Dividetta is a full-time bishop at Gate Agape Ministries in Liberia. Alvin is a preacher in North Dakota. George Parker Jr. is a graduate of African Bible College-Yekepa, Nimba County, Liberia. During my six years in the refugee camp, I served as a pastor, parish president, lay leader, and lay speaker. I have run an online ministry since 2020 on Facebook and YouTube. Everything our family has achieved I dedicate to our mother and our late hardworking father, George A. Parker Sr. Because of them, to this day, we maintain a strong family union that keeps everyone together. May their souls rest in perfect peace. Pray that God continues to bless the works of their hands. I hope their legacies live on and continue among us.

FIVE

Love and Denials

B EFORE THE CIVIL war in Liberia in 1990, I worked with Ash Thompson Memorial Academy as an administrative assistant to her honor Judge- luvenia Ash-Thompson. While sitting in my office one day, I saw a charming and attractive woman enter the building. She had one of the most beautiful smiles I had ever seen. She approached my desk, greeted me, and introduced herself as Miss Annie Wade Hare. She handed me a job application as a kindergarten teacher. I asked her to come back the next day. I gave her application to the principal for review. Miss Hare was asked to return for an interview the next day. I was curious if she would get the job.

I prayed so hard for her to get a job. Before I saw her that day, I was single, looking for true love because the mother of my two daughters had broken up with me for reasons she knew best. When I saw Miss Hare, an electric shock wave ran through my body, filling me with extreme love. I couldn't wait to speak again with her. Whenever I went closer to her, I held my breath and began to snivel internally.

But this was a kindergarten school, and as an administrator, I had to fight hard for self-control. My world floated in a beautiful sky when my new love was near. After all, children are good observers and often understand what is going on between adults more than we realize. She had strong feelings that she couldn't express, but her smiles would pierce my soul. My soul sank every time I saw her. I finally unleashed my feelings for her in one of the sweetest moments of my life, and hopefully hers at the time. I told her, "I truly found the amazing love of my life at this moment." It was unbelievable.

All this was happening during the Liberian Civil War. Rebel forces had besieged the capital, Monrovia. In the fog of the war, I embarked on a journey of love that I had waited for a long time. I didn't know where it would take me; it didn't matter. When you fall in love, you fall into another world where there is patience and kindness, without jealousy, boasting, arrogance, or provocations. You don't have to take into account the evil actions of others. It is a world of love, where all good things are possible.

There is hope in all things. Endure all struggles, and love will never fail. I never realized what agape love was until Miss Hare entered my life. She was everything to me. She had the traits I wanted in a woman since she was a caring, loving person and full of compassion, not just for me, but for everyone who experienced it, including her friends and family.

Prejudice, Personal Experiences, Segregation, Hatred, and Labelling

The scars of the civil war create post-traumatic stress disorder in the lives of so many innocent people. I certainly had my share. I experienced intense pressure from my late father-in-law and my late girlfriend, Annie Wade Hare. Her father felt I did not meet the criterion and status to be his daughter's boyfriend. He considered me a "country boy." He once told his daughter he could not bear to see his granddaughter by the name of Yoryor, who he expected to become his daughter's husband. He wanted his grandchildren to have last names like Cooper, Williams,

Johnson, and so on. And that man had to be wealthy. He was intolerance to my plights of a true love story' yet, I experience such rejection.

But it was not the end of my frustrations. After Annie's death, her office raised about $5,000-Liberian dollars to help with the education of our little girl. To my surprise, Annie's father deprived me of any control over money or access to my daughter. I didn't care about the money because I was heartbroken. I encountered severe hatred.

My little girl got very ill and passed away two months after her mother's death. My late daughter's grandfather extended his hatred by planning to send my daughter to the United States without my consent to isolate me from the family. I received the information later. Shortly after, the little girl I love so much passed away and ended my connection to the late Wade Hare family. Left with psychological trauma and a tortured mind, I took courage from the words of Annie, who often told me, "Isaac, the most important thing between us is love. We love each other. That's all that matters." I often remember these words from inspiration and hope. Even today, they assure me I was not wrong to love her with all my heart and soul.

I know many innocent people discriminated against in their homeland lost their lives. They never had the opportunity to be reassured by their loved ones. I am lucky to have received that security, which I will treasure for the rest of my life. The next chapter expresses the deep emotions that followed the deaths that stole my love and left me shattered.

SIX

Love, Care, and Death of Our Little Girl Two Months after Her Mother's Death

UNFORTUNATELY, ALL THIS joy ended when death took Annie, my dear love, away unexpectedly. She became seriously ill during the civil war and was diagnosed with jaundice. When her condition worsened, I decided to take her to the hospital. There was no public transportation. The only people with vehicles at the time were the rebel forces that roamed the city. The dilemma was how to ask that group of people who never had feelings for human life. It left me emotionally wrecked. I ran down the road, trying to find a way to get her to the hospital. Fortunately, I found a neighbor who took us to the emergency room at St. Joseph Catholic Hospital in Monrovia. She was admitted to the hospital and I went out to find food for her. When I returned, a nurse gave me the bad news. I fainted. The life of my love had ended in the blink of an eye. When I woke up, they took me to see her body in the emergency room. Today, the memory of seeing her lying on that stretcher is still fresh.

My relationship with Annie Wade Hare produced a beautiful girl named Dee. She brought joy and love to her mother and me. We enjoyed Dee for about two and a half years. Then her mother passed away, and I stayed alone to take care of my baby without her loving and caring mother. I struggled to find food and money to buy the things Dee needed. The active war had just subsided, and there was massive looting and theft of personal property. Danger was everywhere in parts of Monrovia. Nobody owned anything. Nothing was safe. I often left my little Dee with her aunt to search for food. If I were lucky, I would run into a friend who gave me money or food that I would take to her aunt.

One fateful day, after two weeks of trying to find food and money in the chaos with armed rebels roaming the city, my daughter's aunt found me in the street. She told me that Dee was very sick, and no one could help. I was overwhelmed with sadness and immediately dropped everything I was doing to help with my sick baby. When I arrived at the aunt's house, I was horrified by Dee'scondition. She was very ill, and I immediately took her to the hospital. At the time, St. Joseph Hospital, a private Catholic hospital, was the only operating hospital in the city. I went to the office crying bitterly and begged the doctors to save my Lil-Dee's life. Unfortunately, I had no money to pay for medicine or treatment. A doctor (Miss Sanvee) was very understanding. She told me to go home and promised that she would take care of the bills for Lil-Dee, which equaled twenty-five Canadian dollars.

Considering the deplorable situation in Liberia, no one had money at that time because the rebels were taking it from anyone. If someone was unlucky, they would take his or her money. Otherwise, they might kill you. I decided to sleep in the hospital that night instead of risking danger from the rebels.

During a restless sleep, I dreamed I saw the mother (the late Annie Wade Hare) of my little girl. The woman appeared in a white dress. She reached out and took our little girl, who wore a cute white dress. Someone behind a counter handed our girl to her mother. I did not recognize the person who gave our little girl to her mom in this fateful dream. Also, I never realized God was showing me a vision. It was like a movie.

The doctor told me my baby had died when I woke up the following day. It was only two months after the death of her mother. I was devastated. Everyone who knew us demonstrated extreme sympathy. I saw in the eyes of friends and family expressions of sorrow for my condition.

The sorrow of the dream vision reminds me of the story of Lazarus, "Now a man named Lazarus was sick. He was from Bethany, the village of Mary and her sister Martha. (This Mary, whose brother Lazarus now lay sick, was the same one who poured perfume on the Lord and wiped his feet with her hair). So the sisters sent word to Jesus, "Lord, the one you love is sick."

When he heard this, Jesus said, "This sickness will not end in death." No, it is for God's glory so that God's Son may be glorified through it."(John 11:1-4-NIV).

The time between the two deaths appeared so unbelievably short that people would forget I was grieving two deaths. When my friends and relatives saw me, they asked, "How is your girl there?" Imagine such a difficult question in times of intense grief. The story above, for me, is a great reminder of who we should look up to in times like these. I would reply, "My girl and her mother passed away." Only those who have experienced a similar loss can understand my feelings.

After these tragic events, I began to understand more about what life was all about and what is essential in our lives. It is vital that as we go through the paths of life, we must always recognize the value that comes with it. We must live correctly.

We sometimes think that life is long. In truth, it is very short. The next chapter teaches us how life transitions from stage to stage along the paths of life. As we live our lives, a feeling of expectation and desire for a sure thing to happen often follows a turbulent path. But life must move on. Even though our expectations might be bleak, we hold onto the true meanings of life.

SEVEN

The Affliction Point and Meeting Evelyn, My First Married Wife

A FTER DEATH ENDED Annie's life, I began dating Evelyn M. Larkpor, who came into my life as what appeared to be a guardian angel. My soul was tired and my body weary from a world of dreams. It was funny how I started to go out with Evelyn. I was experiencing severe financial difficulties, with no money for my upkeep. One day I decided to visit the Providence Corporation, which was owned by Evelyn's cousin, Mr. Benjamin Garnett. Evelyn received me with a big smile, as well as her friend and workmate Barbara Morton. I presented them with my curriculum vitae.

The next day, I decided to follow up. When I got to the office, rather than discuss my application, Barbara Morton started interviewing me, not because of the work, but for personal reasons. She asked questions like, "Are you married? Do you have a girlfriend?" I noticed that Evelyn was smiling during the whole conversation with Barbara. I quickly took the opportunity I always wanted and started to fall in love with

Evelyn. We connected after a couple of visits. I finally got a job, through the intervention of Mr. Garnett's Wife, Igna Sherman-Garnett. Mrs. Garnett's sympathy came as a result of wearing a trouser using rope rather than a belt. In African, using ropes in to hold your trouser up is a sign of an **arid of a desolate impoverished condition.**

Evelyn and I continue dating during the war. My situation was very challenging for me as a man in love. I was responsible for protecting Evelyn by going through bullets and sometimes caught between two forces of combat. In many cases, the battles went on for days and weeks, but we survived. It was destiny.

Separated by war, Evelyn escaped to safety with her family. They left Liberia to travel to the neighbouring Ivory Coast. We met in the refugee camp in Ghana and started a new life together as refugees. Soon she became pregnant and gave birth to our daughter, Islyn. After losing Dee, Evelyn's pregnancy seemed like a miracle. I knew that God had given me the joy I had lost. I named my new daughter after her late sister, Islyn Dwehde Yoryor. I gave my new daughter the middle name Hope. She was named Islyn Hope Yoryor because there was undoubtedly a renewed hope in my life. Everyone knew how much I loved my new daughter. Before Evelyn's pregnancy, I spent many nights crying over the little girl I lost. After Evelyn gave birth to a girl, God answered my prayers. I transferred the love I had for her late sister to my new daughter.

Everyone in the refugee camp in Ghana loved Islyn. I enjoyed the first seven years of her life in the refugee camp simply because I was fascinated and overwhelmed by love. We were protective of her and had many other concerns because we lived in a refugee camp. Although we found ourselves in African settings, we were Christians and spent a lot of time praying. After many years of struggles in the refugee camp, Evelyn and I finally married on December 23, 2002, at the Buduburam United Methodist Church in the refugee camp in Ghana. I served as a lay leader of the church. Because we had Islyn out of wedlock, we needed to get married. Besides, I could not continue to occupy that position in the church without being married. Besides, we were in love.

We had a long and tedious wait at the refugee camp. Our settlement processes to Canada took us two years of working with the Canadian Embassy. "It will be a trip to remember," I told myself. Although we were not working, we had to take shuttle buses from the refugee camp every two weeks to do a follow-up at the Canadian Embassy. Our spirits were no longer in our host country, Ghana. Some days we had to take our food money to go to the city to follow up at the Canadian Embassy near Accra. We knew that in the days to come, our dream of leaving the refugee camp would come true. We counted down the days until we could leave the camp. We were very impatient and anxious to exit the refugee life we had experienced for many years with God as our helper.

Our family was able to travel to Canada in November 2005. We came to Canada with the dream of continuing our education to be able to take care of our family correctly. In addition, we wanted to make sure that our children received a proper education. I understood that age was not a barrier to education. That made it easy for us to attend classes where the other students were much younger than we were. Evelyn and I grew up in the same town in Liberia. Our families did not leave any stone untouched in terms of our upbringing. Our fathers taught us the value of life with the hope that we would apply and teach these values to our children and grandchildren. When we arrived in Canada, I had spent fourteen years at the Liberian refugee camp in Ghana, West Africa. Evelyn was pregnant when we arrived in Canada on November 14, 2005.

Fortunately, we found a good family doctor who told us that Evelyn was pregnant with a girl. It was our first time experiencing having an ultrasound. She gave birth on June 7, 2006. We named our new daughter Andriel MarufaYoryor. She is my fourth daughter. I named her Marufa as a token of gratitude to the general manager of the dissolved Organization of Settlement and Integration (SISO) for her maternal love and concern shown to my wife, Evelyn, who was pregnant, dehydrated, and very pale. She had just come from a refugee camp, and health-care availability for refugees had been lacking. Can you imagine coming from a refugee camp with a pregnant woman in such a deplorable state? However, Marufa Shawreine did everything she could for my wife. She got Evelyn the medical help she needed and made several visits to see how she was doing.

I hoped Evelyn and I would raise our daughters with the same values we had shared over the years; they had become the base of our fortress. Since Islyn was Andriel's older sister, and both lived with us in the same house, it was essential for Islyn to grow up as a role model for her little sister. As a parent, I tried to be firm about what I thought was suitable for her upbringing. It's very different being a father in an African setting, where you see yourself as the overbearing head of your household with the last word. Canada was different. The laws governing parenting are different. Women and children in Canadian culture appear to be the heads of households, quite the opposite of a typical African home. The worst thing is being a parent in a refugee camp. You feel and question your masculinity, especially when you feel incapable of feeding your family. In such a situation, you often feel like you have no control. But I realize that God loves and is close to me.

During my time in the refugee camp, my blood pressure was always between 188 and 200. Seventy-five percent of my life hadbeen very stressful. The situation we found in Canada was difficult because we were in a different social situation and trying to adjust to a new culture. Our values were similar in parenting, but our values and cultures differed during the early days in Canada. Unfortunately, Evelyn and I experienced a communication breakdown when helping and leading the girls. We discovered that thirteen-year-old Islyn wasgrowingup in a difficult partnership with her parents because of the problems Evelyn and I had. I understood. We were always anxious to give our children a good and moral education to support them when Evelyn and I were no longer here. Our fights were mainly over the children. I later realized that as a parent and head of the household, I made many mistakes and misjudgements in handling family affairs because I was not careful about gauging parenting expectations and practices in Canada. I soon realized I was stuck in culture shock.

In two years apart, I never tired of trying to reconcile with my wife, a dream that I finally achieved with the help of my pastor, friends, and the family doctor. It is a challenge being a Christian man or a "Christ-centered man." This is where obedience to God takes effect. At this point, you must choose between the flesh and the Holy Spirit.

God must be my central figure in everything: my decisions, choices, and what I say and do. My general demeanor should reflect my spiritual values, which serve as an example for my family. I think both Christian man and Christ-centered man are reflected in Canada.

EIGHT

The Historical Authenticity of Liberia

I N THIS CHAPTER, I present intricate, detailed historical reflections on the formation of a Liberia characterized by internal conflicts. The scenarios led to the distancing of indigenous Liberia and early political internal strife and segregation. The ramifications of this have followed me throughout much of my life.

In 1816, the formation of the American Colonization Society (ACS) was an initiative of the US government. Some states and some ecclesiastical groups led by great clergymen like John Wesley and William Wilberforce took the initiative to preach against the inhumane treatment of enslaved Africans in America. These men wanted to end the trade of enslaved people in the United States and Europe.

Pioneers arrived along the west coast of Africa between 1820 and 1822 aboard three ships, the *Strong*, the *Mayflower*, and the *Elizabeth*. They settled on a small island called Providence Island. Liberia comes from the Latin word *Liber*, which means free.

The instability began when the settlers formed the new state in 1822. They brought the ideology of their enslavers in North America,

23

which became their way of life. Liberia and its citizens also became a complicated nation and people because of captured enslaved people from mischief slave traders channelled through the transatlantic slave trade. There, in the new colony of the United States in Africa, the experiences and complexities of the diversity of people captured through the interception of enslaved Africans on the sea were brought to the shores of Liberia.

The enslaved individuals were intercepted from human rights abuses, repression, and inhumane treatment. But they were a minority and needed the help of the indigenous people. The newcomers tried to integrate with the natives, but it was difficult. Colonists despised and mistreated the natives, just as enslaved black people suffered in the United States in slavery's early days. At this point, along with discrimination, the orders of the day between the pioneers and the natives, the new nation grew, and segregation became paramount among the colonists. The natives ended up being thought of and treated as inferior. Most of the pioneers were of lighter complexion due to interracial marriages that were the result of relations between enslaved people and enslavers that took place before the end of the slave trade.

The natives began to move inland, trading their land for smoked fish, smoked pork, and gunpowder. They let the pioneers live in their communities. When segregation became widespread, the natives began to fight back. They came at night to attack settlers, killing many, and looting property. Security became one of the main concerns of the pioneers—the free blacks from America accompanied by American agents. Agents of the American Colonization Society (ACS) first ruled Liberia. The natives often pursued the white agents, intending to kill them because they believed they were smoked pork.

The natives lived in a primitive world, which was considered a contributing factor to how they viewed these agents. Americans and some of the settlers contributed significantly to the segregation problems between pioneers and natives. Most of the pioneers were of lighter complexion due to interracial marriages that were the result of relations between enslaved people and enslavers that took place before the end of the slave trade.

The settler population was growing, which was one of the reasons to declare Liberia a state. During the eighteenth century, the French and the English gradually colonized Africa. The pioneers thought it would be a good idea to declare the independence of Liberia. They believed that the love of freedom had brought them home, and they trusted their God that it would bring them freedom and peace. They could no longer afford to be ruled by the colonial powers. In 1847, the colonists declared Liberia independent, and Joseph Jenkins Roberts of Virginia became its first president.

At first, the new government did not include any native Liberians. The natives were not allowed past the second grade in school, and most barely learned to read and write. The natives found themselves living as domestic servants in the settlers' houses. It was not until almost a hundred years later, in 1944, that Liberian president William V.S. Tubman established the policy of unification and integration. Before this period, an artificial stigma existed between the two groups. It was no coincidence that such a deadly fight resulted from these conditions. The next chapter delves into a brewing conflict.

NINE

The Background of the Liberian Civil War

WHAT FOLLOWS IS a summary of the causes of the tragic civil war that claimed the lives of over 250,000 people in Liberia from 1990 to 2003: issues of early segregation between the pioneers and the indigenous people upon the former's arrival from the United States. The civil struggles also caused untold suffering for many more. Since 1847, Liberia has been a one-party state. In 1980, a rice riot occurred due to food shortages during the administration of the late president Dr. William R. Tolbert Jr. This was followed by a military coup and civil war in 1980–1990. For many years, Liberia had been a ticking time bomb, governed by a minority group composed mainly of free men of color known as pioneers, resettled from the United States in 1816,the establishment of the ACS with oversight responsibilities to resettle "free slaves," arrived in the "dark "continent in 1820, and in 1847, the declaration of independence. These pioneers were descendants of Liberia's founding fathers and founding mothers, who had largely returned from the United States thanks to the efforts of the ACS, an organization comprised of clergypersons, human rights groups, and philanthropists.

Since the dawn of the rise of the "Negro-Republic," the nation has suffered huge social gaps and issues of ideological differences and rejections of settlers/pioneers the indigenous people met on arrival. Such bickering led to a socially divisive livelihood. Over the years and decades, these issues gave birth to a nation rife with conflicts, divisions, and poverty, contributing factors to the high illiteracy rates that led to foundational dysfunctions. The following chapters detail my stories and the beginning of a deadly journey through the war.

TEN

Liberia at Blaze: My Deadly Journeys

Image from the Liberian deadly civil war, as Rebel
(small soldiers) besieged Monrovia, 1996–2003.

IT WAS ABOUT 6 a.m. on July 2, 1990, in the city of Monrovia, Liberia, the break of dawn after sleepless nights. My family members and I were awakened by the sounds of heavy bombardments of artillery shells directed at the executive mansion where the president resided. It was approximately five kilometres from Twelfth Street, where we lived.

We hurriedly packed our belongings and started our deadly journey. Little did we know the extent of the harassment and brutal treatment of civilians and displaced persons?

We headed toward the American Christian radio relay station ELWA (Internal Love Winning Africa). We decided to go in this direction because we heard it was safe. We first encountered a splinter group of government soldiers loyal to the late slain president, Samuel Doe. One of my brothers, Theophilus Kollie, was wearing a pair of blue jeans. We had no idea government soldiers were searching for persons wearing blue jeans. With God being our helper, he did not accompany us. But later, Theo and Reginald Thompson were murdered at Liberia's executive mansion. According to a report from family members after the war, Theo and a family friend, Reginald Thompson, were thrown into the late president's hungry "lion's den" at the executive mansion.

Along our fateful journeys, the soldiers asked for IDs; they looked very furious. You could see the redness in the corneas of their eyes and smell alcoholic beverages and marijuana.

We were blessed as one of the soldiers knew me; we lived in the same vicinity. He told his friends to let us go. Of course, most of our belongings were already looted. We did not mind what was taken from us; it was a matter of life and death, something we did not imagine from the beginning of our journey. The soldier advised us to remove all blue jeans from our belongings. We were told the rebels were being identified by blue jeans.

After the groups of soldiers, we entered an area called no-man's-land, an area between a place called "Congo Town" and the ELWA Radio relay station we were headed to in search of an assumed haven. There were no other roads to enter ELWA except through no-man's-land. At this no-man's-land, I felt death at a much closer range. It all happened when astride bullet passed in the proximity of my nose. All I heard was a very swift sound with smells of gunpowder and the heat from the bullet. I fell to the ground as I asked all those traveling with me to do likewise. We were on the ground with our faces turned down. I thought I was dead, yet still alive. The episode lasted about thirty minutes.

We continued our journey to the ELWA relay station, not too far from where we were. As we approached the ELWA, our anxiety grew. It felt like we were suddenly entering a lion's den.

As I previously said, we had heard ELWA was safe. I led my family during our entire journey. Fear began to loom over me when I saw a little boy holding an AK-47 rifle. The gun was longer than he was tall. The rebels wore Halloween-like costumes, some wearing masks. Others wore a bin Laden "fashioned bears." I observed three rebel groups of displaced persons during their deadly journey during the war. The first group always appeared to be the "nice guys." The second group seemed to provide comfort and directed everyone where to go. The first two groups were also highly involved in looting. Then came the third group, the deadly group. Hope had been built by the first two groups, but it was crushed by the third and the apparently hopeless situation it brought. This group brought death and harassment, kidnapped young girls and wives, raped women, forced young boys to join the rebel fighting forces, and executed innocent civilians. Executions were carried out based on tribal affiliations or the accusation of being a government soldier or official.

Worries loomed in the minds of people who once lived in peace and tranquility. Liberia had been a country of love and great hospitality. It was a place where almost everyone knew each other. There were daily exchanges of handshakes, hugging, kisses on cheeks, and faces covered with friendly smiles. Before this civil strife, there was a great deal of the spirit of the "Liberian experience," an experience that can only be interpreted by Liberians and those who have tasted such an experience. Liberia is a unique country, one once seen as beacon of hope for Africa and the world. Liberia fought for the independence of other African nations living under imperialist governments. It was the home for many exiled persons. All hopes dissipated in Liberia during the crisis.

The next chapter discusses lost hopes, an atmosphere of no retreat, but surrounded by your fate, a condition of accepting a difficult situation without trying to resist or change it.

ELEVEN

Separating the Sheep from the Goats: The Evil Judgments

A S THESE NARRATIVES continue, the phrase, "Separating the sheep from the goats," is frequently used by rebel commanders at checkpoints. I guess they never realized who the "goats" really were. However, civilians usually made it through checkpoints setup by rebels. We frequently heard questions like, "What's your tribe?""What's your name?""Are you government soldiers?""Where did you work before?" These questions were asked in some of the most horrifying manners. The interrogations were often conducted with several automatic rifles pointing in your face. Most victims were the elderly, women, and children.

Most displaced people were overwhelmed by fatigue, hunger, thirst, and terrible fear for their lives. These senseless and mean questions certainly determined your faith either to live or die. For example, if your tribe was opposed to the rebel faction interrogating you, you could be shot dead on the spot. It was disheartening that these atrocities were conducted in the presence of children and family members. The remaining family members had no choice but to stand by, and if they dared, cry.

These cruel questions were asked because each rebel faction was searching for enemies, the National Patriotic Front of Liberia, (NPFL), headed by the jailed former president Charles Taylor. They looked or government soldiers, police officers, national security officers (including those working with the government), and the tribal men of the late president Samuel Doe. The rest of the rebel factions searched for rebels and tribal groups loyal to Charles Taylor. Other victims included the Liberians, stereotyped as Americo-Liberians, or Congor People, depending on which opposing rebel factions they encountered along the routes manned by rebels. Charles Taylor's father was from the settlement of Arthington along, the St. Pauls River, Liberia.

People fleeing the war faced other checkpoints as well. Some checkpoints, especially in central and south-eastern Liberia, used human intestines as ropes to stop them. These horrifying checkpoints were often identified by the presence of large groups of green flies. The smell of hundreds of corpses lying along the roadside was common. Rebels referred to the odor from these bodies as "Charles Taylor's Cologne."

As we continued our journey, faith had its role to play in my life. Being a Christian and believer in our Lord and Savior, Jesus Christ, my faith led me to travel with a pocket Bible that read:

"The LORD is my shepherd; I shall not be in want. He restores my soul. He guides me in paths of righteousness for his name's sake. Even though I walk through the valley of the shadow of death, I will hear no evil, for you are with me; your rod and your staff, they comfort me." (The 23rd Psalms, 1-6-NIV)

As my family and I approached a checkpoint, I recited the Twenty-third Psalm, my regular spiritual rite to demonstrate my faith and belief that those who followed me would be saved from the evil committed by such a group of rebels with personality disorders.

Rebels killed people in many ways and manners. For example, they placed individuals' necks on pieces of wood and used machetes to behead their victims. Some individuals were tied between two vehicles and pulled apart. The rebels used evil-restraints named and styled: "tar-bay," a painful method of punishment that sometimes led to death. Victims' hands were tightly double-tied at the elbows behind their backs, and rope also tied hands in front of victims, so the blood circulation would eventually stop flowing through the bodies of thousands of victims. The use of guns was the most superficial manner of killing.

My faith saved me. Those who followed me made it across all the checkpoints. All the streams we crossed along the way were undrinkable because of the hundreds of corpses floating in them.

At Duport-Road, Paynesville, Liberia, more than thirty thousand displaced persons were stopped in an open field a few yards from a river nick named River-Jordan. The name came as a result of an overnight stay near this river. The rebels stopped everyone from crossing overnight. Thousands of displaced persons offered prayers that night.

The scene at this riverside reminded Christians of the biblical story of the children of Israel's final crossing of the Jordan River into the Promised Land. But this was not the case here. Rather, thousands were just about to cross into as laughter house. While on the field that night, some groups started going around with water for sale. I had a dollar and bought some of the water. This water had the best taste ever. To my amazement, someone in the crowd shouted, "The water you just drank is from aseptic tank!" Surprisingly, there were no smells of stale pee or poop. Perhaps this was one of the mysteries of God provided for the thousands of thirsty people, including nursing mothers and sick elderly people.

My first shocker came the following morning. An unknown man and his family were sitting on the ground just next to us. A rebel soldier came up to him and asked him to step aside. As I watched, more than four rebel soldiers descended on this helpless innocent man, shooting his helpless body until he was riddled with bullets. Even now, after twenty-four years, the memories remain fresh in my mind. The emotions that followed the killing will resonate with me in lasting memories.

His wife and children were watching. The rebels warned them, "No one is allowed to cry, or all of you will be killed." His wife held her children tightly close to her, frightened with fears of uncertainties looming in her weary soul. She held her children tightly as she sobbed. It was probably running through her mind that they would all die together. Those within proximity were sobbing, including me, in the spirit of extreme sympathy. At this juncture, life had lost its taste, and the expectancy of death was glaringly obvious.

The so-called separating the sheep from the goats (to judge which people or things in a group are bad and which ones are good) continued that morning. At about noon, a rebel asked everyone to begin crossing. It was sympathetic, a scene of everlasting memories. Mothers traveled with most of their belongings, including children's food, clothing, land deeds, money, and other valuables. These individuals, especially the women, carried very heavy loads on their heads and babies tied on their backs. Consequently, during the crossing, I experienced the most chilling experiences that would be told to generations unburdened about what appeared to be unacceptable. Some women were fascinated with material possessions and would rather save their possessions than their innocent children. The babies they carried were very young; some abandoned their children before crossing the swollen river. For others, defenceless babies drowned on their mothers' backs.

I also witnessed rebel soldiers carrying babies around to find their mothers. Perhaps some of the babies' mothers were killed, while some intentionally abandoned their babies. The rebels started handing abandoned babies to any woman they saw without a child. These women were forced to take an abandoned child. Some children and elderly drowned, and some were carried by current.

We finally made it across the river. When I reached the other side, I didn't see many of the elderly who had been traveling with the group. Many of them died overnight on the open fields and along the bush path. Family members had to continue their journeys without them.

The exodus entered an abandoned mission school called Sore-Clinic near Paynesville City, Monrovia. Sore-Clinic was initially considered a haven. But it wasn't too long before I realized it was as 'slaughterhouse' for the innocent, elderly, government officials, and foreigners who sought refuge in Liberia. For these foreigners, Liberia has been their home for decades. But some met their untimely deaths at Sore-Clinic.

During the exodus, my faith had its roots in the Word of God. As I previously mentioned, I traveled with a pocket Bible. I built my faith in God and the Twenty-third Psalm. And with these assurances, my faith led us through all rebel checkpoints. I silently recited these great songs as we approached these deadly checkpoints. The prayers worked beyond my imagination. Even though I wasn't sure of my spirituality at the time of the war, faith kept me holding on to the Word of God. I saw God's grace unfold before my eyes as some of the most feared rebels were the ones God used to safely escort us through these despicable checkpoints.

As head of the family, I came close to death at this famous Sore-Clinic. Here, God's grace and his mercy found the proximity of death. A group of rebel generals started an interview. They asked for my ID. As they interrogated me, it held onto my faith in God. I began to throw words back at them. One of the female commanders ordered that I be beheaded. An unknown woman appeared from behind the rebels and asked, "Where is your family," to which I replied in a loud voice, "All of these who are behind me." She commanded two armed guards to escort me and the group across all dangerous checkpoints.

Two armed guards approached the so-called safe zone. I vividly remember one of the armed rebels who escorted us from Sore-Clinic saying, "There are many other checkpoints ahead of you. We are not responsible for those. Bye."

"God will take us from here!" I replied.

As he said those words, I continued to recite the Twenty-third Psalm in my heart. As we left the Sore-Clinic area, thousands were left behind. Those people also had stories.

This is my favourite verse from the Twenty-third Psalm, verse 4 (NIV): "Even though I walk through the darkest valley, I will fear no evil, for you are with me; your rod and your staff, they comfort me."

The next chapter details the dreadful conditions and displays of draconian acts of killings in a prominent displaced person camp about thirty kilometres from Paynesville, Monrovia. An influx of Liberians from the capital sought imagined safety there.

TWELVE

The Fendell Displaced Persons Camp, University of Liberia

W E HEADED TOWARD one of the notorious displaced persons camps on the University of Liberia campus in Fendell, Liberia, municipality of Mount Barclay, Careysburg district. As we traveled, I saw several decomposed bodies of children, the elderly, and women. Among some wickedness perpetrated by the heartless rebels was the "fun-to-kill game" with pregnant women during the deadly crisis around Fendell, where the University of Liberia Agriculture College is situated. As rebels saw a pregnant woman approach their check points, they began to argue among themselves about the gender of the child in her stomach. Then they opened the pregnant woman's stomach to find out. These acts of extreme cruelty were unimaginable until witnessed against vulnerable, helpless, hungry, devastated women. Most of the women's husbands were brutally murdered in the process.

I witnessed a scenario that involved a family I knew. As a man was traveling with his wife and children, they were stopped at a checkpoint.

The rebel commander asked the woman to step aside. Then, in the presence of all those traveling along the same road and before the gaze of her husband and children, he pointed an AK-47 rifle at her husband and sexually abused her. He told the children that he would kill them all if they cried. These atrocities occurred regularly throughout our journeys and along the routes we traveled. But we had to keep going. We were lucky to pass through these checkpoints alive.

We finally arrived at the University of Liberia Fendell Campus (ULFC). At this juncture; it was all about tears and telling the story over and over. I saw fear in the woman's eyes whenever the rebels came around. We lived in the same cabin in the ULFC academic building.

As the atmosphere of fear, despair, agony, and stress loomed over the camp, I saw a red Volkswagen Golf decorated with human skulls and bones: three hanging at the front, three at the rear, and three other skulls hanging at the right and left doors. There were twelve skulls on one car. I later learned the name of that car's owner was General Rambo.

T Junction led to the Fendell displaced persons camp, another horrible area, and a killing field. This junction was the last checkpoint before entering the displaced persons camp. The so-called final security checks were conducted to separate the sheep from the goats. That is, they were looking for enemies.

The famous deadly Fendell Campus, University of Liberia displaced-persons camp, T Junction, 1990.

After crossing Junction, we entered the ULFC displaced-persons camp. We met friends who advised us to stay put at the camp. The reasons for the advice included the fact there were too many killings in the area, so it was advisable to stay in the camp until receiving the okay to continue.

Our destination in mind was our hometown, about thirty kilometres from the ULFC. We ended up spending about two months on the ULFC. It seemed like two years. We counted the days and nights that never seemed to end. It was a place of mass human devastation and catastrophes. Among many of the evils committed was "a sinister conspiracy," when some families gave their young daughters to rebels with the hope they would find a daily meal. On the other hand, those who belonged to tribal groups or were government officials, former soldiers, and security officers were considered enemies of the rebel faction.

While on the ULFC, we volunteered with the late bishop Alfred G. Reeves of the Victory Temple Church in Paynesville, Liberia, before the crisis. The late bishop set up a prayer group in his living quarters. His place was where people sought refuge, especially former soldiers, government officials, foreigners, tribal groups, and those sought by rebels to be killed.

The group traveling with me later joined my brother M. Dave Parker and his late wife, Florence Baker-Parker. Florence was a nurse and volunteered with Médecins Sans Frontières (Doctors without Borders) at the ULFC. My brother worked at the time with Bishop Reeves, who also set up a social worker unit. I also became a volunteer. We successfully set up an underground operation to save former soldiers and tribal groups being sought. Our duties were to help these persons escape the camp. We showed them how to disguise themselves and what to say when rebels asked them questions. Some former soldiers were identified by the "marks "of military gear. For example, marks left on the legs by socks and boots and the smell of gunpowder. Some were identified by unscrupulous individuals.

Rebels executed babies in an unspeakable manner. A former school friend I met on our arrival at the famous T Junction told me about a horrific ordeal of a woman accused of being a member of a tribe sought by rebels: "Her young baby was taken from her back and smashed on a wooden electric pole. Another lady's baby was thrown into a pool of hungry alligators owned by the University of Liberia's science laboratory and abandoned during the war."

The children were indeed the greatest victims of the war in Liberia. The children were drugged and used as child soldiers. Some mothers left their children unattended and traveled miles in search of food. The only option these children had was to search for food in garbage dumps. Imagine what this food would look like amid greenflies and poop.

A couple of week's later; cholera broke out at the ULFC. In two weeks, there had been approximately five thousand deaths; the majority were children. Among the dead babies, was my sister Shirley Parker's five-month-old baby. It was an extremely difficult and emotional time for us.

The Famous Adam and Eve Creek at the ULFC

While on this camp, I saw high-salvific women lose their self-esteem and dignity. Women stood in the open to have their showers.

Along the streams were scenes of men and women showering together. Husband dared not to say a word and vice versa. Scenes at these streams were compared to those in X-rated movies. The child soldiers regularly visited the bathing site. They named the area Adam and Eve Creek. Here, displaced persons, especially women, were afraid to go far from the camp. Their anxieties were predicated on not returning to their family members.

In my previous testimonies on my spiritual experience during my family's departure from the city, I mentioned my dependence on the Twenty-third Psalm, another assurance of how God protected my family and me. After two months at the camp, we ventured out, moving from the center to travel to our hometown of Bentol, about thirty kilometers from the ULFC. My first personal experience was that no one felt the urge to eat while traveling. Besides, I did not realize if one stays hungry for a couple of days or a week, one's throat narrows. I attempted to drink water, but I couldn't swallow it. It was the worst pain I had ever experienced except for toothaches.

We entered our hometown one night in September 1990. The first rebel we met, named David gave my entire group a place to sleep for the night. It was in an abandoned house owned by Eva Solomon, known as Cousin Eva, away of referring to an older adult in the community.

Rebels owned every property during the war. During the night, two rebel soldiers came for my girlfriend, who traveled with us, apparently to abuse her. I thought it was the end for me. I swelled with anger and boldness and confronted the two rebels. I dared them to touch my girlfriend. In truth, I forgot to recite the Twenty-third Psalm at that moment. In a state of disbelief, I did not realize God was still with me. To my surprise, and amazement, the well-armed rebels ran away. I later realized it was not my power or the rage I showed the armed men. No, it was the passion of God through whose saving grace ignited fear in the rebels and sent them fleeing.

The chilling revelation of the identity of the rebel who escorted us to safety was another assurance of God's protection. The same rebel escorted us to our childhood home the following day. After he left us, an old family friend asked us if we knew the rebel who accompanied us. We said no. "The rebel you called your friend is the most feared killer rebel in Bentol at this moment," he explained. The friend took us to the place this rebel used as his execution ground, and we saw hundreds of bodies. Among them were some of our friends from long before the war. Our friend narrated the story of the decayed bodies and how these individuals butchered.

We spent a week in our hometown. Then one day, a group of former school friends visited our yard and advised us to consider leaving the town. "A breakaway general from the Charles Taylor faction, General Prince Y. Johnson, is about to attack Taylor's rebels at the University of Liberia, Fendell Campus," one of our friends told us.

With this information, I advised my family for us to leave. There were disagreements. I took my girlfriend, and we traveled to her parents' hometown of Buchanan, Grand Bassa County, Liberia. We spent a few months there before traveling to Danade, Ivory Coast. My girlfriend and I separated, and I went on to Ghana in 1990.

THIRTEEN

Liberia Sets Sail into the Path of Self-Destruction, 1980–2003

THE LONGSTANDING CONFLICT between the natives and pioneers worsened in 1980 when enlisted men of the Liberian Armed Forces overthrew the True Whig Party government. The party consisted mainly of the sons and daughters of the pioneers. The government was overthrown in a bloody military coup by armed forces composed primarily of indigenous Liberians. After the takeover by the army, thirteen men from the extinct True-Whig Party were publicly executed by firing squad on orders from the military junta headed by the late master sergeant Samuel Doe. At that moment, most members of the Liberian military had no more than a high school education; they were second-graders.

The military government ruled for ten years. Most of the remnants of Liberian Americans went into exile in the United States during that time. The remnants of the True Whig Party of the American Liberians also went into exile in the United States and Europe. Members of the military government, called the People's Redemption Council (PRC), seized the properties of the thirteen executed men. The members of the military government divided these properties among themselves during their ten years of government rule. During this turmoil, revenge and reprisals seemed imminent.

Unsurprisingly, many murders occurred and retaliations were prevalent during the fourteen years of active civil war. At the end of the ten years of military rule, there were severe tribal divisions within the military government. President Samuel Doe was from the Krahn tribe in south-eastern Liberia. His friend, the commanding general Thomas G. Quiwonkpa—affectionately referred to as "strong man"—was from north western Liberia and a member of the Gio (Dan) tribe. These two main tribes were involved in the war and revenge killings of innocent civilians. It was apparent: Charles Taylor had no problem getting the support of the Gios due to his affiliation with General Quiwonkpa. Samuel Doe secured the backing of the Mandingos tribes, composed mainly of Muslims. The Mandingos are an official tribe of Liberia.

After the deadly division after the 1980 military coup, several prominent names were connected with the PRC government. Among the members of the PRC government who became victims of the regime they led to power were Nicholas Podier, Thomas Wehsieh, Nelson Toe, and Fallah Varney. These men were very influential in President Doe's military government. The first vice president was J. Nicholas Podier. Accused of plotting to overthrow the Doe government, he was later executed after being stopped at the airport, apparently attempting to leave the country. Thomas Wehsieh was also charged with trying to overthrow the government and executed. Fallah Varney, the general secretary of the PRC government, died in a tragic and suspicious car crash. Nelson Toe also, along with Vice President Thomas Wehsieh.

These incidents were the beginning of the downfall of the Doe regime. As the conflicts deepened, it was clear the country was headed to more bloodshed. During and after the early days of military rule, Charles Taylor, who headed the General Service Agency (GSA), was responsible for all government procurements. Mr. Taylor, the operational head of the government of the People's Redemption Council, suddenly disappeared. A year later, President Samuel Doe affirmed in a nationwide broadcast that Charles Taylor had stolen money from the government and had fled to the United States. President Doe had ordered his minister of justice, Jerkins K.Z.B. Scott, to start the extradition process for Mr. Taylor to return to Liberia to face embezzlement charges. The late slain President Samuel Doe's government requested the United States Department of Justice for Taylor's extradition to no avail. Later, BBC Focus on Africa announced Taylor broke into the jail in America and surfaced at Liberia's Loguatuo border with Ivory Coast-West Africa-December 25, 1989. Chapter fourteen details Rebel leader Charles Taylor's departure from Liberia and the fairy tales of how Taylor was jail in America.

FOURTEEN

Charles Taylor's Departure from Liberia and His Counterclaims

C HARLES TAYLOR WAS arrested by the US government and imprisoned on corruption charges in Liberia. While he awaited extradition to Liberia, he was able to retain the services of former US attorney general Ramsey Clark. When the case reached the US courts, the US government in Liberia, led by Samuel Doe, continued the case. At about the same time, on December 25, 1989, Taylor proclaimed a revolution against the Doe government, and rebel forces attacked from the border of Costa de Ivory with Liberia.

I lived in Monrovia at the beginning of the war and had a friend who worked with the National Security Agency (NSA). The late Mr. Dokieh often brought documents and letters from the executive mansion, the official residence and offices of the Liberian president. Among the documents were Charles Taylor's resignation letters. In a couple of other notes, Taylor defended himself against corruption charges. Taylor explains that when the PRC took over the government of Liberia after the military coup in 1980, the late president Doe accused the dethroned True Whig Party government of rampant corruption. Taylor, General Thomas Quiwonkpa, and other members of the new military government warned against continuing similar practices because the public and the international community were watching. In the letter, Taylor accused President Doe and other PRC members of demanding costly cars and a large amount of money for their personal use. According to Taylor, President Doe and the seventeen members of the PRC demanded and received expensive French cars. They also claimed each PRC member needed a Honda Civic in subsequent meetings, intense discussions, and confrontations at several of his town hall meetings. During the reign of the military government, Taylor and Thomas Quiwonkpa were always on the same side on crucial issues. President Doe also ordered two American-made six-door limousines. The late commanding general, Thomas Quiwonkpa, threatened that if the president ever rode in the limousines, he would call his men to open fire on them.

According to Taylor, the demand that caused the most significant division between them was that the government opened foreign exchange accounts for the seventeen ruling council members and built houses for each one in exchange for turning the country into civilian rule. During this discussion at one of the council meetings, Quiwonkpa and Taylor suggested there should be an election to change the military government. The actions of President Doe and some of the council members embarrassed the new government, which had just overthrown another corrupt government. In that letter, Mr. Taylor did not account for the money, which was in the millions.(President Doe later said it was a million dollars.) Taylor closed the letter by saying he was sick and could not return to Liberia.

As the story circulated in Liberia, General Quiwonkpa lost his job as commanding general for the Armed Forces of Liberia (AFL) and left the country shortly after. In November 1985, he launched a rebel raid from the Nimba County border with the Ivory Coast. The Doe regime crushed this revolt. General Quiwonkpa and several hundred citizens of Nimba County were captured and killed. Supporters of President Samuel Doe and then ate General Quiwonkpa;this disgusting cannibalism was aired on national television. In 1989, Taylor, who had been in jail in the United States, turned up in Liberia along the border with the Ivory Coast, where he officially launched his revolution on December 25, 1989. Most Liberians welcomed this action at the time, but it was a short life. It was apparent that a deadly civil uprising was imminent in Liberia.

FIFTEEN

Forced Labor and Summary Killings in Rebel Territories

A BRITISH HISTORIAN of the late nineteenth and early twentieth century, Lord John Emerich Edward Dalberg Acton, once said, "A person's sense of morality lessens as his or her power increases." Rebel commanders issued orders demanding that young men and women join the rebel army. This was ubiquitous in the rebel territories and similar to what happens when people are forced into slavery. It was an insidious, horrendous act perpetrated throughout rebel-held regions of Liberia between 1990 and 2003. Displaced Liberians were also often forced to join the rebels. Weak and hungry fleeing Liberians had no choice and were usually forced to do many terrible things. These evil acts are at the highest level of human abuse I have ever seen. Sometimes people complain about racism and then do the same things as those who complain to others, including their people. How can we expect people to stop discriminating and repressing us when we can't control these same things in ourselves? Before one can complain about discrimination and racism, you must eliminate these deplorable traits in yourself. No one has the right to use uncivilized acts against the human race, regardless of color, orientation, religion, status, race, or geographic location.

People were forced to become rebel soldiers and do hard physical labor on farms and underground in gold mines and diamond mines. Some worked as servants in the homes of the rebel commanders, which were taken from their original owners. In some cases, the original property owners were killed and their belongings confiscated.

People tried to flee the fierce fighting between peacekeepers and the factions fighting for control. The peacekeepers were trying to protect the capital from the takeover of the rebels. It was very traumatizing for the peace makers. They faced a severe dilemma in trying to protect civilians, especially women and children. Peacekeepers were faced with determining which children were used as child soldiers. The peacekeepers were also vulnerable. Both women and men were rebel soldiers. At the same time, the rebel factions fought each other. The journey to safety was always uncertain. Refugees and some foreign citizens tried to find a safe place for their children and older adults.

As mentioned in an earlier chapter, traveling refugees had to pass through dangerous rebel checkpoints. Rebel commanders established checkpoints to separate the enemy civilians they were looking to kill and to loot or steal their property and money. There was nothing like a secure check point, I went through many. They tortured me and took things from me at some checkpoints. It segregated people passing through the checkpoints, suspecting they were government officials or members of the national security force. Unlucky displaced persons were pushed aside and killed, often in front of their children.

Again as mentioned earlier, if the victim had an attractive wife, a rebel might take her as his own. Girls as young as ten were often taken by rebels as wives or to be abused. Rebels also used these vulnerable girls to entertain themselves. The rebels' husbands and wives were sometimes forced at gunpoint to be abused in front of their children. Some brave refugees preferred to lose their lives rather than submit to evil rebel demands to engage in inhumane acts.

The rebels searched for tribal markings associated with the tribes they wanted to kill. Such marks are common among Africans since, in most cases, Africans identify themselves according to different tribal groups. They also vary from country to country and in each political subdivision of Africa. African traditional identities can be very complicated. In Liberia, for example, the local language one speaks or the tribal marks on their bodies identify individual tribal men and women. Another example would be if you're from Nigeria or Ghana, branded facial tribal marks can determine which tribal group or African country you belong to. In some cases, the marks are very similar.

Rebels were also looking for military marks left by using military gear. People were killed for something as small as a mark on the foot caused by wearing socks. Vengeance was rampant.

Charles Taylor's NPFL was divided into two groups. One group became the Independent National Patriotic Front of Liberia (INPFL), led by General Prince Johnson. His men killed soldiers of the government and tribes associated with the government. It became even more dangerous when both forces began searching for and killing anyone they suspected was related to any of the factions. There were widespread killings as more factions formed and joined the fighting forces, all fighting against Charles Taylor's NPFL.

The international community helping to resolve conflicts believed the objective of these factions was to remove Taylor from power and prevent him from committing atrocities against the Liberian people. However, I believe this was an idea doomed to fail because the seven factions committed unimaginable brutal and inhumane atrocities, mentioned here and earlier in the book, while calling for Taylor's removal at the same time.

I have come to believe that one of the most desperate situations that happens to a person is having to beg for his or her life when there is no apparent hope of survival in a chaotic situation. No one is listening. Your killers have no sense of humanity. All African civil wars are characterized by violent activity driven by superstition and psychological manipulation. The atrocities aimed to in still fear in people and make them believe their oppressors were earthly gods. In reality, they were hideous demons in disguise. The bodies of about 90 percent of those brutally murdered rotted on the ground; except for those the Red Cross picked up. All you could smell were the odors of decomposed bodies. The rebels called the smells of decomposed bodies "Charles Taylor Cologne."

SIXTEEN

Exploitation of the Natural Resources
and Issues of Foreign Interests in Africa

L IBERIA'S CIVIL WAR
not only destroyed human
resources but the country's natural resources as well, which became
the financial strength of the various rebel groups. They conspired with
international money launderers and financial monsters with which they
exchanged weapons for diamonds, timber, iron ore, rubber, fishery, and
gold. The elite rebel population sold body parts and human skeletons
to scientific laboratories in neighboring countries and seized valuables
left behind by fleeing refugees. These weapons and ammunitions
were mischievously transported in vehicles with UN, Red Cross, and
Médecins Sans Frontières(Doctors without Borders) markings. I am
sure that the leadership of the rebels perpetrated these dubious acts.

Interestingly, some sectors of the economy did business as usual
during the war. US companies like Firestone Natural Rubber Company,
the world's largest rubber company, never closed completely. And the
Liberia Agriculture Company (LAC) still secretly operated behind Rebel

lines. These companies continued to work contrary to the US position against Charles Taylor and his resistance against the peacekeeping forces and UN operations in rebel-held areas.

The Liberian Civil War worsened due to the economic self-interests of various factions. It is very disappointing that profits came before atrocities and the suffering of innocent people during these times of war and civil unrest. Superpowers and world leaders should consider the next chapter, which includes information about the misapplication of Africa's natural resources, and help to stop poverty, greed, and corrupt leadership in Africa.

SEVENTEEN

Liberian Refugee Camp, Ghana, West Africa

I ARRIVED IN Takaradi, Ghana, on a fishing boat, about sixty kilometers from the Liberian refugee camp. I went to the center of this town with a painful gunshot wound to my right leg. I was lucky to receive treatment at a Red Cross clinic in the camp. At that moment, there was an outpouring of Ghanaian hospitality. Citizens of all occupations came with food and water. There was a reason for this generosity. Some years before, when Ghana experienced a severe economic recession, it received considerable help from Liberia. The people of Ghana were now returning that good deed. Most of those in the camp felt they arrived there alone by the grace of God. A cargo ship called the *Buck Challenger* came with 17,000 refugees fleeing the fighting in Liberia. The fighting had been particularly fierce around Monrovia, Liberia's capital city. As mentioned earlier, the two factions at war were the INPFL, headed by General Prince Johnson, and the NPFL, led by Charles G Taylor.

Meanwhile, the Economic Community West African States Observer Monitoring Group (ECOMOG), native to the counties of the West African economic community, protected the interim government headed by the late Dr. Amos Sawyer. Peacekeepers were also preventing the rebels from taking the city. Monrovia was teeming with more than one million people, including displaced persons, fugitives, criminals, black market scoundrels, foreign aid workers, and diplomatic personnel. For many desperate souls, it was the only perceived haven.

The *Buck Challenger* was heavily overloaded, and several West African states denied him entry on suspicion that the ship carried ex-combatants, rebels, and other undesirables. The vessel was adrift for two weeks in rough seas and then began to sink. Hundreds of refugees, including women and children, died daily, their bodies thrown unceremoniously into the sea. The Ghanaian government, led by the late former president Jerry John Rawlings, finally granted leniency and allowed the ship to dock at the port of Accra for humanitarian reasons.

Today, many parents and children who survived that ordeal have given up hope of ever seeing their relatives again. Others hope their relatives will find refuge in neighboring countries or other parts of the world. Over the years, a lucky few reunited with their children, parents, husbands, and wives. The Buduburam refugee camp became home to more than 30,000 Liberian refugees and foreign residents, many of whom lived with their families in Liberia before the war. The center was a sad and helpless community that offered little hope. People who had lost their homes, money, land, and loved ones sat looking into the distance toward where their homes and their lives used to be. Despite their discouragement, many camp residents turned to religion, and they put their faith in their Lord and Savior, Jesus Christ. Many formed churches throughout the camp to bring hope to the troubled population. In the next chapter, we discuss some of the challenges experienced by the refugees in the camp. But through God, many were saved.

EIGHTEEN

Working in the Liberian Refugee Camp

F EW PAID JOBS were available in the camp; The few jobs in the United Nations were awarded primarily to host country members. Liberians are restricted only to work in the Liberian Welfare Council. The Liberian refugee organization was responsible for the Liberian refugees' welfare council, components of the camp management team, and the Ghana Police Force presence in the camp.

Many refugees created jobs for themselves by establishing small businesses within the refugee community. Family and friends abroad often raised the money for starting these businesses. Families abroad were committed to helping their families and friends in the camp. There was a lot of empathy among those who had the opportunity to travel overseas. Refugees without relatives or friends abroad often survived thanks to manual labor such as making mud bricks, gardening, transporting goods with wheelbarrows, and shining shoes. There were training schools for teaching skills built by UNHCR, the United Methodist Church(thanks to the generosity of veterans, Missionary of the United Methodist Global Board, Rev. Priscilla LegayGilaydeneh),

WAR CHILD Canada, World Vision, and other nongovernmental organizations, some of those who graduated from the Catholic Church Diocese of Ghana.

These schools were intended to build homes for refugees. Others learned to make furniture such as chairs, benches, and beds. I had a wife and children to feed. My cousin, Samuel Gbottee, and other relatives abroad provided us with minimal assistance. But I often needed more money to buy food for my family. There were times when I walked around the camp looking for cash on the ground, hoping to find some coins to buy a morsel of food. Meanwhile, my wife got extremely pale when our living conditions worsened. She was malnourished, sick, and stressed. I could count her ribs. If we were lucky enough to find food, the children would have it for the day's meal. Sometimes, our stressful situation hindered communication between my wife and me.

Despite our misery, God was good to us in many ways. My sister-in-law, Mrs. Etmonia Moore, who lived in Staten Island, New York, was very generous to us and came to our rescue many times. Here, my cousin Samuel Gbotee, my sister Ida Parker, my sister Jessica, and my friends were awesome in helping us to survive the camp's life before were settled abroad.

Unfortunately, the generosity of others was not enough. In the next chapter, I talk about the many unfortunate circumstances refugees encounter with concerns about insecurities and hospitality exhaustion.

NINETEEN

The Darkest Days of the Liberian Refugee in Buduburam Camp

AFTER FOURTEEN YEARS, Ghanaian hospitality toward refugees had worn out. Pressure was exerted by the host country and by the high commissioner of the United Nations for Refugees in Ghana to force Liberians to return home. Unfortunately, there were no signs of peace and security in Liberia; the government of Charles Taylor had been pressured and threatened by recently formed rebel factions. There were numerous acts of human rights abuse. In May 2004, there was a peaceful demonstration by the camp's refugee community. The demonstrators demanded that the welfare council and UNHCR address suspected issues of fraud in the resettlement programs offered by various embassies to Liberian refugees.

The day after the march, a military fighter plane flew over the camp to demonstrate the power of the government. Subsequently, a military helicopter landed in the middle of the local soccer field. An army general from Ghana got on the plane and spoke threateningly.

Well-armed military paraded through the camps with dogs. All male refugees were rounded up and taken to the soccer field; I was among them. Fully geared war-readied soldiers searched the entire area. We spent all day under the sun scorching in a temperature of 95 degrees Fahrenheit (35 degrees Celsius). Refugee houses were searched while the men held on the soccer fields. Most women and children were at home when the soldiers arrived. However, the Ghana army was well-trained and disciplined and mostly acted professionally when dealing with the women and children in registered households.

In what was likely a plan to remove Liberian refugees from the camp, people appeared in the middle of the night and used spears to stab refugees through the windows of their houses. Other refugees were attacked in the streets. This harassment resulted in more demonstrations. Refugees decided to again demonstrate peacefully and march to the police station. To the refugee's surprise, the police opened fire on them, shooting near their heads. Individuals and less-concerned members of the host country were exceptional. The host and representative of UNHCR were silent on the issues of human rights abuses in the camps. For example, contrary to the Geneva Convention, it is prohibited to use weapons near refugee camps.

These incidents continued even after most of us returned home or traveled abroad. Hundreds of refugees were detained and taken to unknown destinations. The host country's police forces picked some up from the soccer field and deported them. Many had already endured years of hardship and pressure to leave behind what little they had accumulated. And now they had to start all over again.

In 2010, there was another peaceful demonstration. But on another occasion, policemen trying to control the crowd shot and killed a thirteen-year-old girl. The official report says that she died from a bullet wound. The question remains, why do law enforcement personnel open fire on innocent civilians and refugees? I pay tribute to the heroes and heroines of the refugee population.

TWENTY

The Fight against the Odds of Settlement in the Refugee Camp, Ghana

Mr. Yoryor advocates for electricity in the
refugee camp for the safety of its refugees.

AMONG LIBERIA'S
FLEEING refugees who
settled in this camp were heroes and heroines. Some, including myself,
spoke against injustices perpetrated against refugees. I pay homage
to the following comrades: Mr. Folley Jaleba, Roosevelt Tulle, Bryant

Slade, James Fiske, Emanuel Gohleh, the late rep. Madison Gonyon, the late Richelieu Porte, Tyrone Marshall, Rev. Priscilla Legay, Jaiah-Gilayeneh, Rev. Samuel Johnson, John and Amos Conoe, Rev. Kpaddeh, Rev. Nathaniel Sackley, the Chairman Liberian's Welfare Council, Mr. Francis J. Hinnah and many more. Thirty thousand people lived under the umbrella of the refugee camp. There were individuals from all occupations. Some inhabited the camp for more than twenty years. The nation of Liberia has sixteen tribes, and all the tribal people lived in the refugee camp. People from all over West Africa who found refuge in Liberia before the conflict found refuge and safety in the camp. As a result, the camp hada very diverse community.

The camp residents were caught up in psychosocial trauma. Many people never had jobs and were heavily dependent on friends and relatives abroad. This created a lot of stress. To deal with stress, many turned to beer-bars, discos, video rooms, pool tables, and internet cafes. Residents congregated at these places daily, whether they had money or not, and regardless of their situations. Camp dwellers would go to see friends who could offer them some ray of hope and happiness. Here I saw wide evidence of the fact that Liberians are a hospitable and sharing people.

The camp had a wide street called the '18', where many people sat all day waiting for those who returned with money from Money Gram or Western Union. They would ask for a few dollars or Ghanaian cedis (the official currency of Ghana). It was a gathering place for internationalmoney doublers and thieves who traveled far and wide to rob people. They wore flashy gold rings, gold chains, and diamonds. They wore expensive clothes, traveled in luxury cars and trucks, and had bodyguards to carry their bag of money. They were often followed by beautiful girls dressed in mini-skirts and short dresses. Some of the girls were covered with tattoos to attract attention inthe hope of getting financial rewards to feed themselves, their children, and their families. Most of those indigenous moms and dads depended on what they brought in daily. The girls also gathered there forbusiness as usual.

Many people played football to relieve stress. Thousands gathered in video rooms, singing and cheering on their favorite teams and players during the playoffs and finals of the European FA Cup. The war brought people from rural areas to urban areas and then to refugee camps, some had never had electricity. They found television new and exciting.

There aremany horrible stories about how some people gained their money. It was unsurprising to discover there were immoral practices, including drugs and child prostitution. Terrible things oftenhappen when thousands of people group in a small territory without money, work, or hope. The war produced thousands of uneducated ex-soldiers, andmany resorted to armed robbery and violence to survive. Others stayed in the camps because they feared prosecution for crimes in other countries. This helps explain why some remained in the center for twenty-one years. The next chapter details the struggles refugees experienced when they finally returnedto their homes.

TWENTY-ONE

The Quest of Liberian Refugees to Return Home

MOST PEOPLE WANTED to go home, but after losing everything in the war, they could not leave. There was nothing to return to. Many hoped to travel to Western and European countries offering resettlement opportunities. Most of the people living in the camp came from rural Liberia. Villages were demolished. An entire town was converted into a forest with wild animals. During the war, some nefarious groups removed the roofsfrom the houses inthese towns. The house roofing material was brought to the city for sale. The market for these looted materials is called "tay-go-market." In the local vernacular, it means "We will continue to infinity."

Through faith, the refugees are still in the camp. There was something more than the hope of resettlement that kept the people holding on after twenty-oneyears of hardship, frustration, and hopelessness in the center. Despite despair caused by hunger, poverty, disease, war, and civil unrest, most Liberians lived as

Christians. Liberia was founded on Christian principles, and these principles permeated the country until President Doe came to power in a bloody military coup. His administration promptly amended the constitution and changed the clause referring to "religious principles." It was clear to everyone that he was a wolf with theskin of a lamb. Changes in religious principles were made to conform to those of the Islamic faith. Until then, Liberia served as a beacon of hope for Africa, known for its warm hospitality in welcoming and caring for strangers, visitors, and people seeking safety. Liberia granted humanitarian status to political exiles. Churches all over the country werefull every Sunday.

The war was a faith-testing experience for Liberians. However, I also believe that the war was another form of punishment for Liberians deviating from the will of God. But despite the difficulties, the people kept their faith even during turbulent times. Hope and confidence in their religious beliefs kept people holding on. The Liberians who lived in the refugee camp in Ghana were no exception. I lived there for fifteen years. I saw people worship God with true faith, expecting God to deliver them. The center's residents got up every day at 4 a.m. for prayer services. Sunday morning, everyone was in church. Although many people were frustrated and sick, they dragged themselves to church or a prayer group to pray for God's healing; this was particularly true in times of pain. There was always some slight hope that they would find a UN-sponsored resettlement program, especially through nations, foreign governments, or churches that would allow them to find new and better lives elsewhere. Refugees must use their abilities or preferences to decide their destinies. They couldn't choose to go home if they didn't have a home to go to.

Many expected an opportunity that would lead them to a safe place. Those who traveled to new destinations generally tried to help the relatives they left behind in the camp. My honest prayer is that God continues to touch the hearts of people and churches. In the West, who will persuade their governments to continue offering resettlement opportunities for the Liberian refugees who remain in the refugee camp in Ghana?

Liberians stayed in the Buduburam Refugee Camp-Ghana from 1990 to 2024, a period of 34 years. The last batch of Liberians was evacuated from the camp from May to June 2024. I am honored to extend my heartfelt thanks to President Dr. Nana Akufo-Addo, the late President Jerry John Rawlings, and the people of Ghana for their generous hospitality during times of war and hunger in Liberia. May God bless Ghana and African Unity!

TWENTY-TWO

Little Tom's Story: Tragedy and the Rewards of Honesty

Part 1

THIS IS THE story of an orphan named Tom. Tom's parents died in the brutal invasions of his parents' home in Paynesville, near Liberia's capital of Monrovia, in 1990. His three brothers and two sisters were also killed. Tom came from a good family. He was a disciplined child; he respected his elders and stood out for always trying to help those less fortunate than him. Tom is the only surviving family member, alone after his family's massacre.

After the slaughter of his family and many friends, he stayed with the help of one of the villagers who took him by the hand and ran with him toward nearby bushes, saving both their lives. Tom and his friend hid in the bushes for several months, looking for food. When the war subsided, they traveled to another town because Tom's town was burned to ashes. They all loved Tom. He made everyone his family and devoted himself to helping the weak and elderly of the town. He helped senior people do the chores at home and filled barrels with water. Although most people in town loved Tom, some of hismates and acquaintances became jealous of him.

A wise older man had watched little Tom when he entered the village and kept an eye on all his activities. The older man was one of the beneficiaries of Tom's services. As Tom's acquaintances grew more jealous, they began to conspire to get rid of him. This group of evildoers secretly met in the bushes and devised a plan to execute Tom. Fortunately, the wise older man had gone into the bushes to bathe and overheard their plans to kill Tom. Tom's enemies planned to kill him by burying him alive. They thought this would avoid any traces of their wrongdoing. They decided they would kill him the next day.

After Tom finished cleaning and tidying the old man's house, the old man gave Tom something to eat and said, "I have something significant to tell you. Your life is in danger." The older man looked tearfully up at Tom. He drew the boy to him and hugged Tom tightly. Tears ran down his cheeks.

Tom had no idea what was going on. He had never experienced anything like it in his close relationship with the older man he called grandfather. "I've never seen you like this before," said Tom.

The older man agreed. "It's heartache. It's often hard. Hold back your tears when it comes to sorrows like this."

"What's up, Grandpa?"

The older man told Tom to sit and began telling him about the plot to get rid of him. "I will reveal to you the secret of life and survival, which will allow you to defeat the evil plans of your enemies. This secret will live with you even after I die."

"What is it?"

"Tomorrow at noon, your so-called friends will ask you to accompany them to the bushes to hunt. However, once there, they plan to bury you alive. You've noticed they're not as friendly to you as they used to be."

"Yes, Grandfather. I was going to talk to you about that."

The older man told Tom to listen carefully and then revealed a plan for Tom to escape from his assassins. "After digging your grave, your hands will be tied. Don't scream, don't cry, and don't be afraid. When they put you in the grave, roll upside down, as they cover you with the mud. Be very careful. Concentrate. As the mud covers, shake it off, and ride on. By then, they will be very anxious to finish and leave. They won't have the slightest idea what you're doing.

"Again, don't be afraid. Continue adjusting yourself to the top of the mud. When you hear, 'Almost done; let's hurry up,' you will be very close to the top of the grave. But stay still. When you're sure that all have left thegrave, you can shake off the mud and stand up. When exiting the ditch, take the path south of town. Go to the secret place I usually take you through those beautiful folktales. Wait there for me until dark. I'll find you."

Events unfolded as the older man predicted. When Tom escaped from his grave, he traveled the road to the south as the older man had advised him.

The older man did what he had promised. He took Tom to his house. Tom hid there for a month, staying indoors to avoid being in public. Bythat time, the whole town was worried about Tom's absence and started looking for him. The wise older man kept his lips closed during this time and rarely ventured out of his house.

Finally, the time came for Tom to appear. The wise older man told Tom a story to tell anyone asking where he had been. "Say that went to a distant city for a special visit, and that the older man had just returned as well, and he regretted not telling them he was also leaving," The older man said. "But never let people know what you're doing," he added.

Everyone in town accepted Tom's apology. The wise older man also told Tom not to tell anyone about the assassination attempt. He advisedTom to treat his friends and his alleged murderers like he had done in the past. So Tom exhibited the same manners and behaviors he had always shown them.

Part 2

The Vanishing Conspirators

Tom listened and followed the advice he received from the older man. The conspirators were scared and confused. First, they were surprised to discover Tom had escaped. And they were puzzled by Tom's behavior after the near-fatal plot against him. He was as kind as always. He smiled often and continued associating with his alleged killers as if nothing had happened. At first, his former friends were confused and hesitant. Finally, they were terrified of what they did not understand. Why was Tom so friendly with the people who tried to kill him?

After a while, the conspirators couldn't take the pressure. One by one, they left the town. They traveled to a distant unknown land, and their families and friends never heard from them again.

The older man continued to give Tom advice. He said he stood firm and brave and prayed to God for wisdom. He told Tom that he must not allow anyone to hold him back. The wise older man advised Tom that when times were hard, he had to shake off frustrations, keep his head up, stay focused, and persist in his efforts to succeed. He also taught Tom that in this life, people can overcome obstacles and fight evil with their minds and souls. Tom likely remembered the hymn written by Charles Wesley that goes, "On Christ, the solid rock, I stand; all other terrains are sand that sinks."

The wise older man believed that burying someone with mud was an act of repression. He reminded Tom that he could overcome any adversity in life because he could get over the fact his so-called friend's buried him alive. Finally, he instilled in Tom the importance of respecting his elders, his community, his government, and the laws of the land. "Tom, if you do this, I believe you will have a long and prosperous life, and the true meanings of life will become apparent during your life's journeys."

The drama of the assassination attempt remained a secret between Tom and his wise old friend he called "Grandpa. The lesson learn in this emotional story is: "As Believers of God and Jesus We Should love Our Enemies and triumph over adversities in our lives, Amen!

TWENTY-THREE

Nehemiah's Vision: A Community Vision

N EHEMIAH, A TIBERIAN
Hebrew (c.500 BC, *Wikipedia*),
is the central figure in the book of Nehemiah. He helped restore the city
of Jerusalem. My definition of community is a place where people exist
near each other. A community can also be in one's heart. It's what you feel
and what you think. It includes your passions, services, and commitments
to your country's development. I always saw myself as a community-
focused person. As a Christian, my strength is my faith in the Lord, who
advised us to be "guardians of our brother" and to "love our neighbor as
ourselves." This origin is where Nehemiah's strength came from. Even
though he was in exile, he lived a prosperous and good life compared to
many of his Jewish compatriots who were subjected to repression and
forced labor. They had to struggle to find food and other needs for their
families. Nehemiah always remembered his roots. He knew everything
good that happened in his life came from the Lord.

Consequently, he needed to help his homeland and the communities
around him. Nehemiah lived in the king's palace as a favored servant,
attending to the king's needs. Here, Nehemiah was burdened by

thoughts and worries about his beloved homeland. He often agonized over thebroken walls of Jerusalem. The king observed that Nehemiah was pensive and said, "What's wrong, Nehemiah? You look sad. It seems to be a sadness of the heart."

"O King," repliedNehemiah, "can you live forever? I heard bad news from Jerusalem. Some friends returned from there and told me that the walls of Jerusalem weredestroyed. I thought when God favors you, nothing could stand in your way to success. Favor generally serves as a driving force for some or most of our successes in life."

"What is your wish?" the king asked.

"I ask you to give me building materials and men to escort me back to Jerusalem to rebuild the city and walls. Also, I will need you to give me a decree that allows me to reach Jerusalem safely."

The king agreed. "When will you return?"

"If it pleases the king to send me, I'll think about it and give youa definite time."

Meanwhile, the queen sat quietly and listened to the conversation between Nehemiah and the king. She was worried because this was a difficult and emotional time for the king's palace.

As Nehemiah was such a humble person, I consider him to be one of the greatest visionaries of all time. The central puzzle in Nehemiah's compassion for his homeland was his quest togive meaning to the lives of his people in his homeland, Jerusalem. Nehemiah was neither passive nor selfish.

And for my natives, whose wall has been brought down by its people? What more than telling the stories of Liberians? I haven't forgotten Liberia because I am in Canada. I cry many nights for my friends and family members left behind, dying of hunger in the streets while we have plenty of food here in Canada. Nehemiah imagines how need would feel, yet there is plenty of high-profile food to his liking and pleasures and favors from the king's table.

In the conclusion of chapter 23, I am overwhelmed with compassion for my home country, Liberia. The devastating aftermath of war has resulted in widespread suffering and hunger, and I deeply empathize with Nehemiah's internal struggles. Despite his efforts to conceal his anguish, the king notices his change in demeanor and profound sorrow. Reflecting on the previous chapter, I am acutely aware of Nehemiah's intense pain and frustrations. Nonetheless, his superior responds with an extraordinary display of fatherly love. Chapter 24 further ignites my commitment to embody the visions of the late Rev. Dr. William R. Tolbert, Jr.

TWENTY-FOUR

Role Modeling the Life and Legacies:
The Late President William R. Tolbert Jr.

I GREW UP in Bentol, Liberia, the hometown of the late president Dr. William Richard Tolbert Jr., the nineteenth president of the Republic of Liberia. President Tolbert was assassinated in a bloody coup on April 12, 1980, as mentioned previously. Tolbert was one of Africa's most visionary leaders. His vision spread far beyond the borders of Liberia. He engaged his fellow African leaders to make the unity of Africa a reality. He became unpopular with Western nations after delivering a historic address to the US Congress that many considered anti-Western.

As young as I was, I admired President Tolbert in the late seventies and early eighties. I was interested in his policy of education and his plan to eliminate ignorance, disease, and poverty in a country with a 90 percent illiteracy rate and a high level of poverty. President Tolbert advocated that his people strive to achieve full participation and to reach higher heights and self-sufficiency. Tolbert dreamed that Liberians would learn to support themselves instead of depending on the US Rice Program. President Tolbert's Mat to Mattress program encouraged affordable housing for low-income people, especially the indigenous people of Liberia, who made up about 80 percent of Liberia's population in the 1970s and 1980s.

I listened to most of Tolbert's speeches, particularly those on July 26 commemorating Liberia's independence. His speeches demonstrated his intellect and humanitarian concern for all Liberians. Tolbert referred to the youth of Liberia as the "precious jewels" of the nation. He was the first president to spread education in Liberia's various counties and territories. President Tolbert's concern for indigenous children was fascinating to me. A large number of indigenous children lived below the poverty line, and this continues to the present. It made sense to concentrate on developing these precious gems. Matthew 6:21 (NIV) tells us, "For where your treasure is, there your heart will be also."

Tolbert started the first home for children in need, hoping they would be picked up from Liberian villages and given a home with loving Christian mothers and fathers who could offer them renewed hope, a solid education and training, vocational training, and opportunities to earn a living. I see the need for such an ideological vision to continue the worthy humanitarian gestures of Liberia's fallen hero president.

I Dream of Helping Indigenous Childrenin Liberia

I have a vision for Liberia and its indigenous children. Liberia's long and bloody civil wars have negatively affected the nation's human resources and ability to care for its people. In particular, the large number of poor children isa huge problem. I foresee the creation ofvillages of homeless children. They would be complete children's villages built to contain all the amenities of a modern Canadian city. It would have dormitories to house thousands of children and a sports stadium for major sporting events, including basketball, soccer, volleyball, track and field, and swimming.

The children's village would contain public schools, secondary schools, vocational schools, hospitals, theaters, churches, supermarkets, and shopping centers. Well-planned streets will encourage walking and public transport as older children would likely not have cars. Police stations, banks, museums, and so on would all be included in the plans. This city will benamed after a North American town to raise awareness in North America. Theplan would aim to show people less fortunate in Africa what life is like in North America without going through the tedious and often futile process of trying to come to North America. This town could also serve as a tourist area, generate revenue for the economic growth of Liberia, and bring the West closer to Africa. The city would also attract international celebrities and other high-profile personalities.

The city's architectural designs provide holiday destinations for college and university students who want to get away for a breather. They could also include research facilities for anthropology and the environment. The hospital in this city could accommodate medical students who wish to study tropical diseases.

Liberia is an ideal destination for tourists. Surrounded by the Atlantic Ocean, it is a perfect place to host these plans as it enjoys the best weather conditions along the west coast of Africa. Liberia as a nation is a natural tourist site with a beach area that almost goes around the country.

Past dreams and visions may seem unrealistic. One of the many reasons for these visions is that after the establishment of the College of Liberia in the eighteenth century (1800), now the University of Liberia, and indigenous Liberians were not allowed to enroll in the Liberian College or pass the third grade or high school compared to privileged children of Americo-Liberians from the Congor or the settlers' children. I strongly they are contributing factors to the country's continuing high illiteracy rate.

As a community, we can make this vision a reality. People with economic resources could take advantage of these opportunities to invest their funds. Others may give for philanthropic reasons without expecting a monetary return. It encourages people of goodwill to come in and help the less fortunate, provide them with hope, and show these children that they are not alone. This city could hold all of Africa, where most countries are accessible by road. Such a city with goods and services from abroad could save many lives and improve its people's standard of living. Doctors across Africa could benefit from training in its medical centers, thus improving the African healthcare system.

I express my great gratitude to celebrities such as Oprah; Angelina Jolie; Brad Pitt; my "idol" from the country music of the West, Carrie Underwood; and a host of other great and kind celebrities who have extended their helping hands to improve the lives of the least fortunate people in Africa. It is my prayer that you visit Liberia. Liberia was devastated by a deadly civil war, mass killings, and the destruction of property, yet it is gradually growing politically. And it is a nation of vast natural resources, such as gold, diamonds, rubber, fisheries, crude oil, forestry, and the eco-carbon industry.

I began to worry about the future of Liberia in the 1970s. Subsequent events justified many of my concerns. Currently, 90 percent of the population is still illiterate. Liberia needs better-equipped schools with trained teachers. Instead of gifts from international companies to Liberia, I would prefer to see more Liberians trained as doctors, teachers, and engineers.

I intend to accomplish these plans by offering scholarships to professionals outside the country and financial benefits that would encourage them to return to Liberia. However, governments in the past, until the administrations of Tolbert and Doe, imported foreign engineers to Liberia with very high salaries and immunities ranging from six months to a year or more. Regarding the treasury department and comptrollers and financiers in public corporations, accountants were brought in by the government from Liberia from the neighboring countries of Ghana, Nigeria, and Sierra Leone to occupy those financial positions. The Tolbert administration inherited most of these devious politics and tried to correct them before the evil forces overthrew their governments.

Foreigners and international communities are drawn to countries with good governance and security. However, Liberia needs the help of many people of goodwill from the international community to achieve these goals. These visionary thoughts became more apparent when I arrived in North America.

I have experienced life for myself. Through my experiences, I realized what it means to have a system of government in which everyone is accountable for their actions when dealing with malpractice and misappropriation of government money, sanctions, and accountability. The most desirable situation is for workers to be paid periodically (for example, every two weeks). Compared with the officials of most African nations—especially my native Liberia's civil servants, who wait three or four months or more for a single salary because the government lacks funds—more of these countries' monies are in the pockets of corrupt government officials. Wage distribution in Liberia worsened after the 1980 military coup. Corruption has overshadowed Liberia because of the high rates of illiteracy.

Individual Liberians have created a culture of extreme dishonesty. Most young people who graduate from college or vocational-technical schools plan to get a piece of the pie. Part of my vision for Liberia is to encourage advocacy for resource use by natives of the country to give all Liberians a right to enjoy the nation's fruits. I often wonder why a country with such a small population (little more than three million people) and vast natural resources of gold, diamonds, oil, timber, iron ore, rubber, and fisheries is experiencing such high poverty ratings. Over the years, governments have failed to raise Liberians' living standards, except for the late president William R. Tolbert. Other administrations have come to do more to raise the standard of living of the suffering masses. A country so rich in resources should not depend on the handouts of international agencies and the United Nations. Liberia is on the list of the most miserable countries in the world.

Liberians have experienced many setbacks in the past. To mention some of these incidents, Firestone Rubber Corporation was established in 1926 after Robert Firestone and the Liberian government signed an agreement to purchase one million acres of land at one cent per acre. The accord pact was to last one hundred years. Firestone provided jobs for the illiterate, underpaid, pampered Liberian elite or indigenous people with the rice program. The next chapter discusses the rice program and its effects.

TWENTY-FIVE

The US Government's
PL-480 Rice Programs

LIBERIA TODAY HAS a history of being the largest rubber plantation in the world without a single factory to produce just a simple plastic grocery bag. There is not only the exploitation of natural resources but also human resources. Firestone is one of the reasons Liberia has such a high illiteracy rate. Illiterate Liberian parents would prefer their children to be rubber tappers instead of attending school.

My father worked for the Firestone Rubber Plantation in the late 1950s. In the fifties and early sixties, he told us how the company gives a worker an increase in salary and additional rice rations for having a male child. The Firestone Company expects the worker to train the male child as a "gatherer rubber" to replace his father or mother. He also told us that the most prevalent disease was a large testicular disorder caused by carrying heavy loadsof latex.

My father also told us a strange story about why he left Firestone. He heard from his friends that when you retired from Firestone, they gave you an "injection unknown" that won't let you live long. He said, "Which is why the company will have to pay you for life." I have always treated this as a rumor.

Apart from rubber, Liberia is rich in iron ore used to produce steel. Mount Nimba, which extends into Guinea, is the ore deposit of the richest iron in Africa. The Liberian side of the mine was actively operated until 1980 by Bethlehem Steel Corporation, a US-based company, and another iron ore company (LNIOC) previously owned by a US company in Bomi County, Liberia. With these huge iron ore companies, there was not a single company producing steel rods for building houses and providing employment to the masses.

Another dream is to see a reduction in corruption in Liberia and other African countries whose citizens suffer from corrupt practices. I would like to see the United Nations pass a resolution supported by the Security Council for the establishment of a corruption crimes court under the Court of Criminal Justice. This court would try African leaders and others suspected of stealing and squandering money that belonged to the country and its people. Money stolen by corrupt individuals in Liberia was transferred to foreign offshore banks. Where was the money hidden? Competent courts of their respective countries try suspects. If found guilty, they would require that illegally obtained funds be repaid to the countries and organizations from which they were stolen. These suggestions are based on the assumption that international criminal tribunals would have the power to transfer stolen money from international banking institutions to the owners of the assets. An authentic government can leverage these suggestions through bilateral agreements. Anyone declared innocent of the charges will be allowed to keep the funds. These courts and judicial procedures serve as deterrents to stop part of the chronic corruption in Liberia and other parts of Africa.

On a positive note, Liberia can rapidly build an effective development program job to help many people. Now that dual citizenship is achievable, Liberia would have long-term economic benefits, allowing well-established Liberians in the diaspora to invest freely in their country of origin through labor resources and business ventures. Unfortunately, the Canadian citizenship we currently have from time to time is counterproductive for us. A Canadian friend who once lived on social assistance told me that my citizenship was just a piece of paper. I replied, "Sir, the Canadian government doesn't think that way." The idea of dual citizenship should not be a big deal.

It could also benefit all parties through transfer business, especially banking institutions. As a point of clarification, there are also clauses in the Liberian constitution granting the right to own land is restricted to people of black descent. I would like to see an amendment passed that would give voting and property rights to all Liberians. Citizens of other countries should also have the right to own land in Liberia.

Let's take Canada as an example. People came here from dozens of other countries, purchased land, property, and businesses, and contributed significantly to Canadian prosperity. To cite one example, Frank Stronach (born September 6, 1932) is an Austrian and Canadian businessman and politician, and the founder of Magna International, an international automotive parts company based in Aurora, Ontario, Canada, Granite Real Estate, and The Stronach Group (*Wikipedia*). He came to Canada from Europe with nothing. He worked in a tool shop and then started his own business (Magna International), which eventually employed thousands of workers. Today, it is worth USD 1.2 billion.

Besides economic and political changes in Liberia, it would also be necessary to establish or restore defense pacts with the United States, Canada, Great Britain, France, China, and Israel. These countries could offer financial, military, and technological assistance to Liberia. Such aid could catapult Liberia into the twenty-first century.

TWENTY-SIX

Bridging the Gaps

FOR MANY REFUGEES, the decision to remain in the camp for a long time was justified. They saw their names on the list of people authorized to leave. For most, this period was the most emotional time of their lives. However, joy and relief were mixed with uncertainty. Some people got so excited that they hallucinated. Joy flowed through the hearts and minds of the families like an electric current. It was also a time for Christians to pray and thank God for his deliverance. Many non-Christians performed thanksgiving rituals, which included the slaughter of goats, chickens, and cows bought thanks to the generosity of relatives abroad.

Things got tough during the last few days my family was in the refugee camp. We couldn't afford food and depended on friends, family, and church members for sustenance. It felt like God had turned his back on us. However, we knew this was not the case, so we waited patiently like many families. Finally, the United States approved our immigration application; unfortunately, thousands of refugee visas were cancelled after the 9/11 terrorist attack on the United States in a tragic twist of the destination. My family's visas were among those cancelled. Once again, it felt like God abandoned us.

We continue to have faith in God and to hold on. Finally, the US government, through the US National Security Agency, referred our cases to the Canadian government through United Nation's High Commission for Refugees (UNHCR), because we had a genuine issue for settlement abroad. Fortunately, the Canadian government granted asylum for reasons of humanitarian aid. The process took about two years. Finally came *the* day. A great deal of stress was removed from our lives, and we began to plan our live-in Canada. We were still determining where we were going to the UNHCR to ask for guidance. It's difficult to explain how we felt at that moment, but *relieved* and *hopeful* are two words that occurred to me. At this point, I had to overcome my fears. I've always been afraid to get on a plane and never dreamed of flying somewhere. I always told myself that if I had the opportunity to travel abroad, I would prefer a boat.

TWENTY-SEVEN

An Emotional Exodus to Canada

T HUS BEGAN THE strangest adventure of our lives. We counted the days and hours until our departure. Along with our feelings of joy, we also felt sadness at having to leave our friends, our beloved church, and the modest but familiar home we had lived in for so many years. However, we had many reasons to be happy to go. We remembered how we had to throw the water out of our room when it rained because we couldn't buy the alpha sheet to cover the roof. We remembered sadly the times we were apprehensive about finding food the next day.

We still shudder when we remember the steps we had to take to protect ourselves against disease and violence. As our departure approached, our worries melted away and were replaced by the joy we felt—joy and anticipation. I remember being so excited that I didn't feel hungry or thirsty. When we arrived at Accra airport for our departure, I had to face my fear of flying. I was about to embark on a very long and stressful flight with my family. My fear intensified when I saw the huge plane parked on the runway. It looked to me like a giant monster about to devour me. I remembered the biblical story of Jonah: "The word of the LORD came to Jonah son of Amittai: "Go to the great city of Nineveh and preach against it, because its wickedness has come up before me."(Jonah 1:1-2-NIV).

Apart from the dissimilarity of the expression of fear, I realized there could be no going back. Returning to the refugee camp was not an option, whereas Jonah had no choice but to obey God's commands and assignments. It was a case of no retreat, no surrender. Canada was our destination, and I had to move on.

My other fear was getting into the elevator. I never thought of getting on an elevator because of the bad experience at home where the elevators needed to be adequately staffed by sufficiently trained maintenance personnel. Our native Liberia lacks constant electricity, and people get stuck in the elevator for hours before they are rescued. Unfortunately, my first apartment had six floors, but I had to overcome my fears.

After boarding the plane, I drank wine and gin, hoping it would make me sleep. Unfortunately, that idea didn't work. I was awake and very highly strung. Fortunately, the children were all delighted, excited, and curious. They had no idea how much their dad was suffering. Because the food on the plane was extraordinary for us, my grandson had a massive bowel movement. Since we had never flown, we needed to figure out what to do. How could we get rid of the dirty jeans he was wearing and clean it up? We also got scared because we thought it might be illegal for a child to poop on the plane. Fortunately, we met two friendly Canadian women. We explained that we were refugees on the way to Canada and described our grandson's plight. They were very understanding. They helped my grandson clean up and showed us the bathroom on the plane where we could dispose of the excrement. We started enjoying the usual Canadian hospitality of these two Canadian women, Miss Montgomery and Miss Duchene. That grandson, Bob Isaac Mariah, enrolled at McMaster University in Hamilton, Ontario, on September 9, 2023.

We stayed in a hotel for about a week before the settlement office found us permanent lodging. Fortunately, the office found an apartment in Villa Marie, 57 Forests Ave., Hamilton, Ontario. In my first experience in a hotel, I went to the toilet and was afraid to use the towels in the bathroom. I thought it was exceptional to see very sparkling white towels. Everything was extraordinary after living in a refugee camp for fifteenyears. We lost our sanities before our miraculous arrival in Hamilton, Ontario.

CONCLUSION

Nomenclatures of Liberia's "Warring Factions

I saw evil unfold, a melodrama, and the narratives about the fourteen-year civil war in the West African state of Liberia, founded by free slaves in 1820, as mentioned previously. The free slaves are also called "settlers." The settlers declared Liberia's independence in 1847. In 1863, President Abraham Lincoln issued the Emancipation Proclamation, freeing the remaining slaves in the United States. And 143 years after its independence was declared, a deadly civil war emerged in Liberia in 1990.

A succession of deadly outbreaks of hostilities between rebel factions occurred in the following years. December 25, 1989, was the beginning. Operation Octopus took place in 1992, and on April 6, 1996, the West African peace monitoring groups (Ecomog) tried to protect the capital of Monrovia from being overrun by Charles Taylor's rebel forces. In 2003, coalition forces led by rebel factions opposed to Charles Taylor moved on the city of Monrovia in a quest to remove Taylor's government from power. The factions included Liberians United for Reconciliation and Democracy (LURD), the United Liberation Movement (ULIMO-J, led by the late Roosevelt Johnson), ULIMO-K (directed by the late Alhaji G.V. Kromah, former information minister, under the administration of the late president), Samuel Doe's National Democratic Party of Liberia (NDPL),the Lofa Defense Force (LDF, headed by the late François Massaquoi), and the Movement for Democracy in Liberia (MODEL, a second anti-Taylor rebel group that invaded southern Liberia in early 2003 and quickly conquered most of the south). The Liberia Peace Council (LPC) was a rebel group that participated in the Liberian Civil War under the leadership of George Boley. The LPC wasformed in 1993, partly as an alternative force for the Armed Forces of Liberia in supporting the fallen former president, Samuel K. Doe.

Taylor, reduced to controlling only a third of Liberia and under pressure from the siege of Monrovia, resigned in August 2003 and fled to Nigeria. The warring parties supported the West African peace mission: Nigeria, Ghana, the United Nations, and the international community headed them. According to the United Nations, approximately, 250,000 lives were lost during these deadly wars. You have read my eyewitness account of what I saw and experienced in 1990 and how the various warlords left rivers of innocent tears in the country known as a beacon of hope for Africa and the world.

Burying the Bones

I was inspired to write these stories based on repetitive revelations to me by my grandmother. I would one day bury her when I grew up. "Burying the Bones" is a personal story that reminds me of "In Flanders Field" (Dr. John Mccrae), a place where the "poppies grow." This poetry is about a fallen friend during World War I, where great men of valorous dignity lie in the fields of splendorous honor. "Burying the Bones" is about the Liberian war and the deaths of weak and innocent souls. These narratives remind us of Liberians, communities of the world, our foreign friends who sought refuge and residence in Liberia, and families wrecked by civil strife. I attempted to allow the world to understandthe spoils of war. The war took away friends, parents, grandparents, brothers, sisters, in-laws, and so on. These are stories of those who involuntarily laid down their lives, the war, and the emotions that follow after survivors return home from various refugee camps in exile. The history included in my story is intended to give you, my audience, the opportunity to understand the historical background of Liberia, its diversities and legitimacy, and words and phrases not familiar to you, my cherished audience. Besides, the stories are written empathetically in African settings, cultures, and traditions. Acquiring a copy of this work and your comments will help improve subsequent publications. This experience will resonate with me all the days of my life and with you. I was distraught and emotional as I penned these experiences that left scars on my heart.

I plan to return home to bury the bones of loved ones found in abandoned and burned towns. Family members located these graves after the war subsided. I have hope and aspirations to honor my grandmother's wishes of being the one to bury her in days to come. But dreams never materialized, and our family could not conceal her bones. Many days and nights of endless tears! I will return to bury her bones, God willing. Genesis 50:25(NIV) tells us, "And Joseph made the Israelites swear an oath and said, "God will surely come to your aid, and then you must carry my bones up from this place."

In the case of many refugee families, burying relatives' bones could not be completed without reflecting on the Buduburam Refugee Camp in Ghana, West Africa, one of Africa's largest and most notorious refugee camps. It was notorious in the sense that the camp was compared to the story of Sodom and Gomorrah. Thousands of Liberians died in this camp between 1990 and 2005; 2005 was my family's last year in the camp. Many Liberians are still in that refugee camp, hoping to travel abroad someday. Some individuals are the only surviving relatives alive and can't bear to return home.

I am unsure if those thousands of graves in an area given a Nike name by Liberian refugees as Area Z would make it home for the burial many Liberians had hoped to achieve. The above sentiments result from the graves being mined for sand by the locals. They began exterminating the refugee cemetery long before my family left for Canada.

The sorrows of reburial are the sorrows of the heart, mind, and soul driven by memories that never go away. It is always fresh in our memories, a daily mirror before our presence. Those with relatives buried in Area Z have no hope but know they can lean on Jesus' name and God's grace to share memories of fallen loved ones. Liberians are well known for celebrating Decoration Day. The destroyed cemetery comprises 90 percent of those who died in the Buduburam Refugee Camp.

Many Liberians put much effort into sending their dead relatives home. Thousands of other families could not afford it at the time. I assumed those relatives who buried their relatives in a nearby large city called Winiba, Central Region, Ghana, may be lucky to transfer the bones of their dead relatives.

During my stay in the refugee camp, I served as a leader for the local United Methodist Church congregation. I recommended and arranged for many burials in Winiba through the city's municipal government. I used the word "lucky" in the previous paragraph because, during my many visits to the cemetery in Winiba, I recorded lots of graves, if not all, opened, no casket or human remains. The scene was very puzzling to me. I asked the lady who often accompanied me to negotiate for burial permits why the graves were open. "There are disgruntled fishermen who use the bodies to fish," she explained. "When they set the nets for a catch overnight, the bodies are used as bait to attract certain fish. Consequently, not all the bones will return home."

I spoke with my brother Amos Kollie, who confirmed that many Liberians returning from exile were burying the bones of their loved ones. Many people remember where they left their weakened grandparents and relatives along bush paths and in villages where they once lived. The bones of the dead souls who could not complete the journey lay in the previously mentioned areas. Here, I am calling on all well-wishers and people of compassion around the world to end war and the suffering of impoverished people of Africa.

A Call to Action for International Communities Regarding Bilateral Agreements: A Deterrent to End War and Corruption in Africa

I firmly believe in deterrents and better-defined rules for collating ideas on using foreign aid in war-weary Africa. Furthermore, it would discourage corrupt African governments and individuals. In addition to monitoring foreign assistance to Africa and third world countries, there is an urgent need for the United Nations and the United States—in conjunction with the African Union (AU) and the Economic Community of West African States (ECOWAS)—to make it illegal for industrialized nations, large corporations, and individuals to fuel wars in these African countries, which has become a site for mass graves, toxic wastes, and tests of deadly weapons. During the 1980s, through law enforcement officers, the Liberian government disposed of drums of toxic wastes repeatedly discovered along the Liberian coast; information about these toxic materials aired on the national news. No one knew how poisonous materials were in Liberian territorial waters. I think Africa and other poverty-stricken countries are unstable because it is easy to infiltrate an individual or a group of people when there is disunity due to instabilities. Eighty percent of African countries suffer from corruption, nepotism, and political strife.

Furthermore, because African countries suffer destabilization, famine, drought, and poverty, dishonest and corrupt individuals are in government, and public corporations distribute the country's money in their pockets and enrich foreign banks, especially in postwar Liberia. I hope the United Nations can pass a resolution to embargo these bank accounts and return said money to the embezzled countries. These actions would deter corrupt individuals in these countries so the poor and devastated would survive. If war crimes were transferred to the International Court of Justice, it should be good enough to take corrupt individuals to The Hague to answer corruption charges. If they are found guilty, illegally acquired money should be confiscated and returned to the countries in question, and the appropriate punishments meted out for perpetrators if found guilty. These individuals should serve terms behind bars. For decades, Liberia has suffered malpractice through rampant corruption in public corporations and legal institutions.

The world must unite to fight for the vulnerable people in Liberia. Liberia suffers an 80 percent illiteracy rate. Such social degradations are the result of great humiliation brought about by loss of status, reputation, or self-esteem. The issues of profit marginalization by foreign investors should be monitored by the United Nations and countries like the United States, Great Britain, and the European Union. Corrupt officials in Liberia should be caged in The Hague as a deterrent and save African/Liberian economic security for the less fortunate. All agreements between foreign investors in Africa should be monitored by the United States, Great Britain, the United Nations, and all industrialized nations in order to end poverty and eliminate corrupt individuals from African governments. For example, whenever there are wars in Africa and other parts of the world—like Russia's war in Ukraine and now Israel and Hamas—weighted economic pressures are placed on all superpowers. We can collate our views as people of the world to end the crises that bring much suffering to vulnerable people and all warring nations around the world.

As I conclude, the following topics express my compassions and the way forward ideas and suggestions to finally end the thirty-four years of the civil uprising and one of Africa's deadliest civil wars characterized by the use of child soldiers, massive looting of Liberia's natural resources, and crimes of human degradations such as extreme abuses of women and underage children/girls forced to maturity. Liberia is surging into an intense and controversial establishment of war crimes and economic crimes courts. Liberia has suffered greatly from massive corruption and extraordinary human rights abuses during the fourteen-year war and the administration of outgoing president George Weah, who lost to the Hon. Joseph N. Boakai.

Hopes and Aspirations for the Recovery of Liberia from a Deadly Crisis

President Joseph Nyemah Boakai of Liberia finally pounced on the controversial issues of the war and economic crimes courts in Liberia. Joseph Nyumah Boakai(born November 30, 1944) is a Liberian politician with more than forty years of experience working in government. He is Liberia's twenty-sixth and current president. He served as the twenty-ninth vice president of Liberia from 2006 to 2018, under President Ellen Johnson Sirleaf, and as the minister of agriculture from 1983 to 1985. Boakai ran for president in 2017, losing to George Weah. He went on to defeat Weah in the2023 election.

After the cessation of the active war in Liberia, and through the immense efforts of the civil liberties and the international community's headed by the United Nations, the United States, Great Britain, ECOWAS, and the AU, alongside The Hague, sponsored the Truce and Reconciliations Commission headed by veteran Liberian lawyer Jerome J. Vedier Sr., Liberia's leading human rights activist and environmental lawyer. The Vedier Commission approved the establishment of the War and Economic Crimes Court in Liberia.

The Realities of Liberian Society

Introduction: Understanding the complexities of Liberian society is crucial as it provides insights into the dynamics of our social, political, and economic systems. It also sheds light on the influence of social media, its impact on public discourse and awareness, and its role in shaping public opinion and promoting dialogues.

Significance of Talk Shows and Influence on Public Sentiment and Decision-making: Talk shows inform the public about current events and developments and hold government and institutions accountable.

The Function of the Senate and the House of Representatives: This includes legislative processes and decision-making, as well as the representation of constituents' interests.

County Administration and Governance: This involves the management of local affairs and resources, and its impact on community development and welfare.

Addressing Major Issues, we must confront allegations of corruption and the challenges posed by money-driven interests in order to seek transparency and accountability in public office, reassuring the public and instilling confidence in our governance. We must also focus on empowering Liberian citizens, fostering civic engagement and awareness, and encouraging active participation in shaping the country's future leaders after such a devastating civil strife. The country is still lagging behind in rehabilitating former child soldiers and their parents.

Conclusion:

I strongly believe that processes of empowering Liberian citizens, fostering civic engagement and awareness, and transforming the lives of ex-combatants are still absent in post-war Liberia. God bless America and the countries who are striving give our nation a "Helping Hand."

APPENDIX

Citation Information:

Yoryor, Isaac. "How We Can "Bell the Cat": African Canadian Perspectives of the Canadian Child Welfare System." Journal of Law and Social Policy 28:2. (2018): 97-105.

https://digitalcommons.osgoode.yorku.ca/jlsp/vol28/iss1/16

Former Liberian Refugee
Camp-Ghana-1990-2024

Mr. & Mrs. Isaac Alexander
Yoryor Marriage Ceremony-2003
Liberian Refugee Camp-
Ghana, West Africa

Alexis & Valerie Yoryor

Isaac Yoryor, *Giving Life Meaning*
Isaac's story of his 15 years spent inside a Liberian refugee
camp was one of the most tragic personal accounts
we've ever read. We knew from the first paragraph
that his story needed to be heard by as many people as
possible. We wanted to see his commitment to turning
his experience into life wisdom to its best possible
conclusion. Undoubtedly, Isaac's story – and that of the
Liberian people – will eventually be read by thousands.
(http://openbookeditors.com/success_stories.html)

ABOUT THE AUTHOR

Isaac Alex Yoryor was born in 1963 in Liberia, West Africa. In 1984, he graduated from Frank E. Tolbert High School, Montserrado County, Liberia, and later enrolled in the Booker T. Washington Vocational Institute in Kakata, Liberia, where he studied auto mechanics from 1985 to 1986. Mr. Yoryor enrolled in the Institute Lincoln Commercial and studied accounting shortly after arriving in Canada.

Mr. Yoryor is a writer and a publisher. His works include Canadian Child Welfare System(Issues of "Systemic Racism"), and he was a contributor to the *Law and Social Policy* (JLSP; Osgoode Hall, School of Law, York University, Toronto). He also initiated publishing a book on the history of founding members of the refugee church at Buduburam United Methodist Church, Ghana. Mr. Yoryor enrolled at Mohawk College in the technician program for automotive energy. Mr. Yoryor also studied health care and graduated from the Personal Support Worker Program at Mohawk College.

In 1990, Mr. Yoryor fled the civil war in his native Liberia to the Ivory Coast and Ghana. He lived in the Buduburam refugee camp for fifteen years and served Buduburam United Methodist Church in various capacities, including as pastor, parish chairperson, lay leader, and lay speaker. Mr. Yoryor initiated many projects, including a computer school and an elementary school under the auspices of Rev. Priscilla Legay Gilayeneh. He also wrote a history book for the United Methodist Church in Ghana detailing the church's founding. His book describes the hard work of the founding mothers, fathers, and pastors, one who was later a bishop emeritus for the United Methodist Annual Conference Liberian.

While in the refugee camp, Mr. Yoryor volunteered in social work and served as general secretary of the council of elders. Mr. Yoryor married Evelyn Larkpor Moore. His marriage was blessed with two girls, Islyn and Andriel Yoryor. Mr. Yoryor also has two older daughters, Valerie and Alexis Yoryor, and a son, Daddy Boy Yoryor. In 2009, Mr. Yoryor and members of his family became Canadian citizens.

While in college, he volunteered in the international education program at Mohawk College and as a peer mentor. From 2007 to 2009, he participated in a workshop sponsored by the Department of Social Services at McMaster University in Hamilton. He also lectured a class of fifty-four students at McMaster UniversitySchool of Social Work, Hamilton. Mr. Yoryou was honoredto speak at the Children's Aids Society, Hamilton, Ontario.

Mr. Yoryor was elected church secretary at Philpot Memorial Church in 2010 and volunteers as a greeter and usher there. Mr. Isaac Alex Yoryor-III is a ministries/Christian studies graduate of McMaster University Divinity and Seminary-2020, Hamilton, Ontario-Canada. Mr. Yoryor holds over thirty certificates of merit for his services at the Liberian refugeecamp, Ghana, and in Canada.

McMaster University Divinity
College-2013-2020

Alexis & Daddy-Saniquille,
Nimba county-Liberia-2018

Printed in the United States
by Baker & Taylor Publisher Services